REGENTS RENAISSANCE DRAMA SERIES

General Editor: Cyrus Hoy
Advisory Editor: G. E. Bentley

THE CITY MADAM

PHILIP MASSINGER

The City Madam

Edited by

Cyrus Hoy

UNIVERSITY OF NEBRASKA PRESS · LINCOLN

MANUFACTURED IN THE UNITED STATES OF AMERICA

Regents Renaissance Drama Series

The purpose of the Regents Renaissance Drama Series is to provide soundly edited texts, in modern spelling, of the more significant plays of the Elizabethan, Jacobean, and Caroline theater. Each text in the series is based on a fresh collation of all sixteenth- and seventeenth-century editions. The textual notes, which appear above the line at the bottom of each page, record all substantive departures from the edition used as the copy-text. Variant substantive readings among sixteenth- and seventeenth-century editions are listed there as well. In cases where two or more of the old editions present widely divergent readings, a list of substantive variants in editions through the seventeenth century is given in an appendix. Editions after 1700 are referred to in the textual notes only when an emendation originating in some one of them is received into the text. Variants of accidentals (spelling, punctuation, capitalization) are not recorded in the notes. Contracted forms of characters' names are silently expanded in speech prefixes and stage directions, and, in the case of speech prefixes, are regularized. Additions to the stage directions of the copy-text are enclosed in brackets. Stage directions such as "within" or "aside" are enclosed in parentheses when they occur in the copy-text.

Spelling has been modernized along consciously conservative lines. "Murther" has become "murder," and "burthen," "burden," but within the limits of a modernized text, and with the following exceptions, the linguistic quality of the original has been carefully preserved. The variety of contracted forms (*'em*, *'am*, *'m*, *'um*, *'hem*) used in the drama of the period for the pronoun *them* are here regularly given as *'em*, and the alternation between *a'th'* and *o'th'* (for *on* or *of the*) is regularly reproduced as *o'th'*. The copy-text distinction between preterite endings in *-d* and *-ed* is preserved except where the elision of *e* occurs in the penultimate syllable; in such cases, the final syllable is contracted. Thus, where the old editions read "threat'ned," those of the present series read "threaten'd." Where, in the old editions, a contracted preterite in *-y'd* would yield *-i'd* in modern spelling (as in "try'd," "cry'd," "deny'd"), the word is here given in its full form (e.g., "tried," "cried," "denied").

Punctuation has been brought into accord with modern practices. The effort here has been to achieve a balance between the generally light pointing of the old editions, and a system of punctuation which, without overloading the text with exclamation marks, semicolons, and dashes, will make the often loosely flowing verse (and prose) of the original syntactically intelligible to the modern reader. Dashes are regularly used only to indicate interrupted speeches, or shifts of address within a single speech.

Explanatory notes, chiefly concerned with glossing obsolete words and phrases, are printed below the textual notes at the bottom of each page. References to stage directions in the notes follow the admirable system of the Revels editions, whereby stage directions are keyed, decimally, to the line of the text before or after which they occur. Thus, a note on 0.2 has reference to the second line of the stage direction at the beginning of the scene in question. A note on 115.1 has reference to the first line of the stage direction following line 115 of the text of the relevant scene.

CYRUS HOY

University of Rochester

Contents

Abbreviations

Bailey   N. Bailey. *An Universal Etymological English Dictionary.* 13th edn. London, 1749.

Bentley   Gerald Eades Bentley. *The Jacobean and Caroline Stage.* Oxford, 1941–1956.

conj.   conjecture

Cotgrave   Randle Cotgrave. *A Dictionary of the French and English Tongues.* London, 1611.

Coxeter   *The Works of Philip Massinger.* Ed. Thomas Coxeter. London, 1759.

Dodsley   Robert Dodsley. *A Select Collection of Old Plays,* Vol. VIII. London, 1744.

Gifford   *The Plays of Philip Massinger.* Ed. W. Gifford. London, 1813.

Kirk   *The City-Madam.* Ed. Rudolf Kirk. Princeton, 1934.

Lilly   William Lilly. *An Introduction to Astrology.* London, 1939. (A reproduction of Lilly's *Christian Astrology.* London, 1647.)

Mason   *The Dramatick Works of Philip Massinger.* Ed. John Monck Mason. London, 1779.

Nares   Robert Nares. *A Glossary; or, Collection of Words, Phrases, Names, and Allusions to Customs, Proverbs, &c. which have been thought to require Illustration, in the Works of English Authors, particularly Shakespeare, and his Contemporaries.* London, 1822.

OED   *Oxford English Dictionary.*

Onions   C. T. Onions. *A Shakespeare Glossary.* Oxford, 1911.

Q   Quarto, 1658–1659.

S.D.   stage direction

Strype   John Strype, ed. *A Survey of the Cities of London and Westminster . . . by John Stow.* London, 1720.

Tilley   Morris Palmer Tilley. *A Dictionary of the Proverbs in England in the Sixteenth and Seventeenth Centuries*. Ann Arbor, 1950.

Wheatley   Henry B. Wheatley. *London Past and Present, Its History, Associations, and Traditions*. Based upon *The Handbook of London* by Peter Cunningham. London, 1891.

Introduction

DATE AND AUTHOR

According to the office-book of Sir Henry Herbert, Master of the Revels from 1623 to 1642, Massinger's *The City Madam* was licensed for production on May 25, 1632. The date has been questioned. In the prologue to Massinger's *The Guardian* (licensed October 31, 1633) occurs the statement that "After twice putting forth to sea, his fame/ Shipwrack'd in either, and his once known name/ In two years silence buried, perhaps lost/ I' the general opinion," the author will try again. The implication would seem to be that Massinger's last two plays had been failures, and if the 1632 licensing date for *The City Madam* is correct, then it would have been one of these. Those who, like Fleay and the play's most recent editor, Rudolf Kirk, find it improbable that the play should not have met with favor when first produced, regard it as an old play revised and licensed anew in 1632, in which case the two plays which had bid fair to wreck the dramatist's fame, alluded to in the prologue to *The Guardian*, could have reference to such of his more recent efforts as *The Emperor of the East*, *Believe as You List*, or the now lost *The Unfortunate Piety*, all licensed in 1631. Professor Bentley, on the other hand, finds nothing improbable in supposing *The City Madam* to have been an initial failure, though he accepts the 1632 date "with some doubt."[1] But the King's Men regarded the play as a sufficiently valuable item in their repertory to take steps for protecting it from the printers in 1641, as Professor Bentley points out; and the prologue to *The Guardian* might have been attached to that play at any time during the twenty-year period between its licensing in 1633 and its publication in 1655, and so in fact have no bearing on the date of *The City Madam*. The evidence, such as it is, is much too vague to bear any certain interpretation, and in the absence of any other contemporary references to the play or its performance, it can only be assigned to 1632, with whatever reservations.

[1] Gerald Eades Bentley, *The Jacobean and Caroline Stage* (Oxford, 1956), IV, 773.

By then, Massinger had been active in the London theater for nearly twenty years. Born in Salisbury in 1583, the son of Arthur Massinger, a gentleman in the service of the Earls of Pembroke, he attended Oxford, where he matriculated at St. Alban Hall on May 14, 1602, but took no degree. Anthony à Wood says that Massinger was "encouraged in his studies by the Earl of Pembroke," but that "he applied his mind more to poetry and romances for about four years or more, than to logic and philosophy." [2] We first hear of him on the London theatrical scene in an undated letter, written presumably in the summer of 1613 by the actor-dramatist Nathan Field to the theatrical manager Philip Henslowe. Field, Robert Daborne, and Massinger, together with John Fletcher, were jointly writing a play for one of Henslowe's companies; but the first three named were in debtors' prison at the moment, and Field wrote to implore Henslowe for an advance of five pounds to bail them out. To Field's request, Daborne and Massinger each subjoined an appeal of his own ("I have ever found you a true loving friend to me, and in so small a suit, it being honest, I hope you will not fail us"—so runs Massinger's.) [3] Two years later, Massinger was still having dealings with Henslowe; he signed a bond, together with Daborne, on July 4, 1615, for the payment of three pounds to Henslowe on the first of August following. [4] But in the years that immediately followed, he began to write for the King's Men, London's principal acting company—the company for which Shakespeare had been the chief dramatist until his retirement in 1611, and whose reigning dramatist now was Fletcher. Massinger's association with Fletcher had begun at least by 1613, to judge from Field's aforementioned letter to Henslowe. It was in this year that Fletcher's former collaborator, Francis Beaumont, retired from the theater, and in the years that followed, Massinger became the new partner to the senior dramatist. During the next decade, most of his work was done in collaboration with Fletcher and others, although at least five plays of his unaided authorship (*The Duke of Milan*, *The Bondman*, *The Parliament of Love*, *The Renegado*, *A New Way to Pay Old Debts*) survive from this period. After Fletcher's death in August, 1625, Massinger succeeded him as the regular dramatist for the King's Men, and produced a steady

[2] Quoted in Bentley, IV, 751.
[3] *Henslowe Papers*, ed. W. W. Greg (London, 1907), p. 66 (spelling modernized).
[4] Greg, p. 85.

sequence of plays over the next fifteen years. He was, indeed, one of the most prolific dramatists of the period; his name is connected— either as sole author, collaborator, or reviser—with nearly sixty plays. Of these, fifteen survive as his unaided work. He is present in nineteen of the fifty-odd plays loosely attributed to Beaumont and Fletcher.[5] Apart from his association with Fletcher and company, he collaborated independently with others: with Field in *The Fatal Dowry*, with Dekker in *The Virgin Martyr*, with Middleton and Rowley in *The Old Law*. Some twenty of his plays have been lost, and are known only as titles from entries in Herbert's office-book and the Stationers' Register. He died in London, and was buried at St. Saviour's, Southwark, on March 18, 1640. Anthony à Wood says of his death and burial: "He made his last exit very suddenly, in his house on the Bank-side in Southwark, near to the then play-house, for he went to bed well and was dead before morning. Whereupon his body, being accompanied by comedians, was buried about the middle of that ch. yard belonging to S. Saviours church there, commonly called the Bull-head ch. yard, that is, in that which joyns to the Bull-head tavern. . . ."[6]

THE PLAY

Comedy, by definition, is concerned with representing the ridiculous, a point that is stressed in all Renaissance critical pronouncements on the nature of comedy. The statement of the Italian critic Trissino (in his *Poetica*, 1529) is typical: "Comedy is an imitation of the wicked and the vicious, yet not in every extremity of the vices, but merely of that which is ugly, whence springs the ridiculous, which is an ugly defect without pain and without deaths."[7] Statements to this effect are to be found in virtually every Renaissance critical treatise in which the nature of comedy is considered, and they all go back to Aristotle's assertion, in the fifth chapter of the *Poetics*, that "comedy is an imitation of those who are worse than ourselves, yet not in every sort of evil but only in that baseness of

[5] For an account of Massinger's collaboration in the Beaumont and Fletcher plays, see my "The Shares of Fletcher and His Collaborators in the Beaumont and Fletcher Canon," *Studies in Bibliography*, Vols. VIII–IX, XI–XV.

[6] Quoted in Bentley, IV, 757.

[7] *Literary Criticism, Plato to Dryden*, ed. Allan H. Gilbert (New York, 1940), p. 224.

which the ridiculous is a species." [8] Concerning the nature of the
ridiculous, and in what it consists, the most explicit statement in
English literary criticism comes in the eighteenth century, in Henry
Fielding's preface to *Joseph Andrews* (1742). "The only source of the
true ridiculous," Fielding there declares, "is affectation," and
affectation, according to Fielding, proceeds from one of two causes,
vanity or hypocrisy. It is a discerning judgment, valuable alike in
considering comedy in general, and Massinger's comedy of *The City
Madam* in particular.

Vanity and hypocrisy are, in fact, the dual themes with which
Massinger's play is concerned. The vanity of Lady Frugal and her
daughters has its parallel in the hypocrisy of Luke, and it is the
purpose of the comedy to expose each for the affectation—shallow,
vicious, ugly, in a word, ridiculous—that it is. Incongruity is of the
essence in comedy, and nothing is more incongruous, or more
ridiculous, than the spectacle of men and women seeking to pass
themselves off for what they are not. Luke, in *The City Madam*,
affects sundry virtues—piety, humility, charity—when in truth he
is a blackhearted scoundrel. The wife and daughters of the middle-
class London merchant, Sir John Frugal, affect the manners and
the dress of the nobility, and expose themselves as thorough vul-
garians in so doing. In both cases, appearances fail to square with the
underlying truth of character, and the comic objective will be to see
that they do. The ladies must be made to recognize the folly—to
give it no worse a name—of their vanity, and Luke must be revealed
for the hypocrite that he is.

The moral aim of comedy is to correct manners and morals by
exposing folly and vice to the withering scorn of laughter. This
view of the purpose of comedy is a commonplace of Renaissance
criticism. "Comedy," says Sir Philip Sidney in *The Defense of Poesie*
(1583), "is an imitation of the common errors of our life, which [the
comic dramatist] representeth in the most ridiculous and scornful
sort that may be, so as it is impossible that any beholder can be
content to be such a one." [9] The hardheaded rationale underlying
this premise would appear to be that if men and women will not
conduct themselves in a seemly manner from love of virtue, they
will at least maintain a hold on propriety out of fear of appearing
fools or worse. When, at the end of *The City Madam*, the vanity of the
ladies has been humbled and the perfidious Luke has been put to

[8] *Ibid.*, p. 74.   [9] *Ibid.*, pp. 431–432.

shame at the height of all his devious scheming, we have a prime instance of the manner in which comedy serves as a curb to folly and vice by depicting—"in the most ridiculous and scornful sort that may be"—the ignominious ends to which they lead. The comic dramatist becomes thereby a figure of no small importance in administering to the well-being of society. His job is twofold: (1) to inculcate an ideal of moral virtue and rational good sense and (2) to let fly with all the satiric and ironic shafts at his command against the excesses of vanity and greed which are forever threatening to upset the ideal moral and rational balance.

The moral function of art, specifically of the comic art, implicit in all that has just been said, is traditional, and it is inherent in all Renaissance critical doctrine. But Renaissance critical theory never forgot the injunction of Horace, which decreed that the poet was to provide moral instruction in a pleasing manner. He is to teach, but he is also to delight, since whatever he may have to say of profit will be more palatable, and more readily administered, if it is turned out in a fictional guise—complete with an arresting variety of incidents and personalities—from which an audience can derive pleasure. The theory which holds it to be the poet's duty to instruct and to entertain at a single stroke is evident in the practice of Elizabethan and Jacobean comic dramatists such as Jonson and Chapman, Middleton and Massinger. When Massinger, in *The City Madam*, ridicules the ladies of Sir John Frugal's family for their efforts—vain in every sense of the word—to ape the style of the gentry, he is, at one and the same time, setting before us an amusing piece of satiric portraiture, and making a perfectly serious social and moral criticism.

The vanity of the women is offensive because, in their pride, they have assumed airs inappropriate to their social rank, and in so doing have shown themselves plainly discontented with the station in life in which heaven has seen fit to place them. The women of *The City Madam* are, in a minor way, in revolt, and Sir John Frugal is no longer master in his own house. They are in the process of usurping the prerogatives of men, even as they have appropriated—though they have in no sense assimilated—the fashions of the nobility. The hypocrisy of Luke, on the other hand, is not only offensive, it is also dangerous, principally because, as Milton was to say, hypocrisy is "the only evil that walks/ Invisible, except to God alone." Neither man nor angel is proof against its wiles. The provident Sir John has his suspicions about his younger brother, the sometime prodigal who has run through his inheritance and is now reduced to living off the charity of Sir John, and enduring the insults which the latter's wife and daughters heap upon him. But Lord Lacy is charmed when, with Luke's conniving, he overhears that gentleman intercede with his brother in behalf of the debtors—Penury, Fortune, Hoyst—and in the process say some eloquent things on the subject of charity, the virtues of which he has learned about the hard way. And the prentices, Goldwire and Tradewell, hail Luke as one of their own when he shows himself of one mind with them concerning the propriety of dipping into the master's till for funds to pay their gambling debts and entertain their whores. Even the ladies, his erstwhile tormentors, are taken in for one heady moment, after he has been named the administrator of Sir John's fortune, by his grandiose promises to advance the splendor of their state.

He proves, in fact, their tormentor, humbling them as they had previously humbled him, but to a significantly different end. Here we see the manner in which Massinger joins the issue between the dual themes on which his play is built. Hypocrisy becomes the scourge of vanity. Luke descends upon the women like some heaven-sent affliction, punishing them for their past arrogance, castigating the folly of their presumptuous affectations, and the end is that they are brought to recognize the error of their ways, and to repent of these. Working the women to repentance has not, needless to say, been Luke's first aim, but then scourges are typically but the instruments of a higher purpose. He may glory, as he says on one occasion (IV.iv.60 ff.), in the power he has "to scourge a general vice" by forcing the women to act and dress in a manner becoming to their station in life, but his foremost concern is with holding on to the fortune which, as he admits (V.iii.24–26), "dissimulation" alone has brought him; and if he does not succeed in sacrificing his sister-in-law and his nieces to the pagan dieties of the colony of Virginia, it is not because he doesn't try.

By the end of the play, he has been weighed in the scales and has been found lacking. Massinger employs a familiar plot device for testing Luke's honesty, one which Shakespeare had used to similar purpose in *Measure for Measure*. Announcement is made of Sir John's retirement to a monastery, whither he has repaired in despair for the outrageous behavior of the ladies of his household, and he designates Luke his heir, with complete authority over the administration of his fortune. But like the Duke Vincentio in *Measure for Measure*, his absence is only apparent. He remains on the scene in disguise to observe whether the power which money brings can change the purposes which Luke has professed, to discover—in the words of the Duke concerning Angelo in Shakespeare's play—"what our seemers be." And so, although a Luke or an Angelo may plot busily, and fiendishly, to work their wills on others, and to safeguard their positions at every step of their devious way, their plots are doomed to come to nought, even as they are doomed to exposure in the end, since the power that put them where they are is watching and judging their every move, and can be depended on to come to the aid of their victims before they can do their worst. Claudio, in *Measure for Measure*, is not beheaded, and the ladies of *The City Madam* are not dispatched to Virginia. The irony of the last three acts of Massinger's play consists in large part in the audience's awareness that the manipulator of others is himself being outmaneuvered; and Luke takes his place in the gallery of Elizabethan comic schemers who, like Marlowe's Jew of Malta and Jonson's Volpone, find themselves hoist with their own petard.

The characterization of Luke is Massinger's crowning achievement in this play. If the individual strokes which contribute to the portrayal of this Elizabethan Tartuffe are recognizably imitated from the work of Massinger's predecessors in the art of comic portraiture on the English Renaissance stage, the total conception is nonetheless remarkably bold and original. From one moment to the next, as Luke's character unfolds, he may echo the accents of Jonson's Volpone, as when he dwells in poetic transport on the contents of his brother's countinghouse, which he has just seen for the first time, in his soliloquy at the beginning of III.iii; he may conjure up memories of Shakespeare's Shylock, as when he warns Lord Lacy to look to his bond (V.ii.79); at his most outrageous, when the mood of unenlightened self-interest is most fully upon him, he reminds us of no one so much as Marlowe's Barabas.

> I am well,
> And so I surfeit here in all abundance,
> Though styl'd a cormorant, a cutthroat, Jew,
> And prosecuted with the fatal curses
> Of widows, undone orphans, and what else
> Such as malign my state can load me with,
> I will not envy it.   (V.iii.30–36)

Language of this sort had become a characteristic means of .portraying the miser on the English stage by Massinger's time. His own Sir Giles Overreach, in *A New Way to Pay Old Debts*, speaks in a similar vein. There is a sense in which Luke, in his avarice and his hypocrisy, becomes a comic parody of the typical Machiavellian villain of Elizabethan drama. He gives a ready assent to the remark, voiced by Sir John in his disguise as a godless American Indian, that there is "no religion, nor virtue/ But in abundance, and no vice but want" (III.iii.106–107), which comes very close to the dictum, pronounced by Machiavel himself in the prologue to *The Jew of Malta*, that religion is but a childish toy and there is no sin but ignorance. Later in the play, Luke is heard bidding "Religion, conscience, charity" adieu; declaring that for him they are "words only, and no more"; and affirming that all human happiness consists in wealth alone (IV.ii.131–133). He congratulates himself on the fact that the felicity he has come to enjoy has been gained, not

> By vows to saints above, and much less purchas'd
> By thriving industry; nor fall'n upon me
> As a reward to piety and religion,
> Or service for my country. I owe all this
> To dissimulation, and the shape
> I wore of goodness. (V.iii.21–26)

Sir John, at the end of the play, is right to denounce him as an "avaricious atheist" (V.iii.135).

What is original in Massinger's conception of Luke is the character's dramatically plausible development from prodigal to miser, from humble servant to tyrannous master. Typically in Elizabethan drama, villainy is a given in the character of the villain. If he has ever been otherwise, we do not know it, neither are we afforded much insight into how he came to be the way he is. With the character of Luke, all is clear. He has been a spendthrift in his youth, which was a mistake; he has learned the hard way; and when he comes into the possession of wealth once again, he is prepared to hang onto it. Nothing is more revealing on this score than the extent of his miserliness. He is loath to celebrate his birthday on account of the cost, though he savors the delicacies that are provided at someone else's expense ("How sweetly/ These dainties, when unpaid for, please my palate!"); and a principal motive in his decision to pack the women off to Virginia is that they eat too much. If his beginnings fail to justify his end, at least they help to account for it.

His felicity collapses, ironically enough, just when he is enjoying it most. He is seated, all at his ease, at the birthday feast which Sir John, still in Indian disguise, has provided; viewing the spectacles—the masque of Orpheus, the *tableau vivant* of his victims kneeling to him for mercy—which Sir John's supposed diabolic art has conjured up as so many appeals to his benevolence, and showing himself proof against them all (Orpheus' music may move the powers of hell but not the heart of Luke); and savoring the sense of his own bliss, which is the more sweet by comparison with the misery he is in the process of inflicting on others. Regularly in English Renaissance drama, the villain is confronted with his fate in the midst of revelry. The maskers, who are his enemies in disguise, enter at the height of the feast to entertain the company, but throw off their masking robes at the appropriate moment to confound the villain with their presence, and to take an appropriate vengeance. So it is in plays like Marston's *Malcontent* or Tourneur's *Revenger's Tragedy*, where what is introduced as a diverting spectacle turns into a very present threat that must be reckoned with. In the final scene of *The City Madam*, the sundry spirits whom Sir John has presumably raised with his supposed magic are so many breathing victims of Luke's vindictiveness; the portraits of Lacy and Plenty take on life and step down from their frames; and the presenter of this whole highly contrived occasion, Sir John himself, throws off his own outlandish disguise, to the confusion of his brother. Hypocrisy is put to flight, and vanity is cured, as Lady Frugal is reconciled to her husband, and the daughters to their suitors. Good sense prevails over the folly and the vice that have flourished for a season, and the comedy ends, appropriately, on the note of forgiveness to all. Even Lady Frugal is heard interceding with her husband on behalf of Luke,

> Because his cruelty to me, and mine,
> Did good upon us.

It only remains for Sir John to sum up the moral of the play, as this applies to the civic virtues of seventeenth-century London.

THE TEXT

The City Madam was not printed until eighteen years after Massinger's death, when a quarto edition appeared. The title page reads as follows:

The/ City-Madam,/ A/ Comedie./ As it was acted at the private House in/ *Black Friers* with great applause./ Written by *Philip Massinger* Gent./ [ornament]/ London/ Printed for *Andrew Pennycuicke*, one of the Actors,/ in the year 1658.

The printer, although not named on the title page, was Jane Bell, as Kirk demonstrated through the identification of the ornamental headpiece which appears at the top of sigs. A2 and B1.[10] Variant title pages, some bearing the date 1658, others dated 1659, are to be found among the copies of the quarto that survive. All extant copies dated 1659 are dedicated "To the truly Noble and virtuous/ Lady *Ann*, Countess of *Oxford*." Copies dated 1658 are dedicated, variously, to Lady Ann; "To the truly Noble/ John Wrath/ Esquire"; "To the truly Noble/ Thomas Freake/ Esquire"; "To the truly Noble/ Richard Steadwell/ Esquire"; "To the truly Noble/ Mr Lee/ Esquire." In addition to the press-variant headings to the dedication, that to Lady Ann required changes in the address ("Honoured Sir!" being altered to "Honoured lady!" at line 3) and in the subscription ("Sir," being altered to "Madam," at line 21). Pennycuicke, the actor for whom, according to the title page, the quarto was printed, was engaging in a familiar racket: the dedication of a book to multiple patrons in the expectation of receiving multiple payments from the individuals thus honored. In dedicating *The City Madam* to five different patrons, he was apparently emboldened by his success in a similar venture of two years before. The edition of Dekker and Ford's *The Sun's Darling* (also printed by Jane Bell) which he and another actor, Theophilus Bird, published in 1656–1657 (copies of the play exist with title pages bearing the alternate dates) was dedicated, variously, to the Earl of Southampton, the Earl of Kingston, the Earl of Northumberland, and Lady Newton.[11]

Copy for the quarto of *The City Madam* was very clearly a manuscript that had been used as a theatrical promptbook. This is evident from the number of anticipatory stage directions, wherein properties are readied for use in later scenes (as at I.ii.144–148 and II.ii.10), musicians are cued (as at III.i.4–5 and V.i.7–11), and actors are alerted to prepare themselves behind the scenes (as at V.ii.69–70 and V.iii.44–45). Directions such as these are regularly printed in the margin of the quarto. They are given in the textual notes to the

10 Rudolf Kirk, ed., *The City Madam* (Princeton, 1934), pp. 8–11.

11 Fredson Bowers, ed., *The Dramatic Works of Thomas Dekker* (Cambridge, 1961), IV, 3.

present edition. The general fullness of the play's stage directions of a non-anticipatory kind suggests, however, that the promptbook was prepared from Massinger's own manuscript. Such a stage direction as the long, descriptive one at V.iii.59 is far more likely to have originated with the author than with the bookkeeper. So with the direction which brings Lady Frugal, Anne, and Mary on stage, "in coarse habit, weeping," at IV.iv.23, and the earlier one which prescribes weeping at II.ii.209. The direction after the next line, according to which Lady Frugal breaks Stargaze's head and beats him (II.ii.210), is of a piece with those at III.i.46–47, whereby we are told than Shave'em "draws her knife" and Ramble "his sword": here, as elsewhere in the text, the dramatist can be detected fitting the action to the words. And the Latinate stage direction, "*Exeunt omnes praeter* Luke" (at I.ii.104), would point directly, even if nothing else did, to an author's manuscript behind the quarto text.[12]

There is also the evidence of the list of "Actors' Names" attached to the quarto. Here the character who, throughout the text, is regularly called Sir John Frugal, is named Sir John Rich; and the younger Lacy is named Sir John, though he is called Sir Maurice on the two occasions in the play (I.ii.78 and 90) when he is addressed by his Christian name. One can only suppose these to have been Massinger's original names for the two characters, and that at some point before the play went into production, he saw the inadvisability of having two Sir Johns, and recognized the ironic propriety of naming his wealthy merchant Frugal instead of Rich, by way of pointing the contrast between the husband's thrift and his family's extravagance. Goldwire alludes to just this point early in the play (I.i.32–33).

The present edition is based on a collation of six copies of the 1658–1659 quarto (the only seventeenth-century edition): Bodleian copy 1 (Mal. 185[4]), copy 2 (Mal. Q23), copy 3 (Mal. Q57), copy 4 (Mal. 237[5]); Folger Shakespeare Library; Library of Congress. Alterations were made in the text while the sheets were passing through the press. Corrections, in substantives and accidentals, have been found in the outer forme of sheet D, the inner forme of sheet G, and the outer forme of sheet K, among the copies collated. These, as concern substantive readings, are recorded in the textual notes.

[12] For additional evidence that the play was set from an authorial manuscript, see A. K. McIlwraith, "The Printer's Copy for *The City Madam*," *Modern Language Notes*, L (1935), 173–174.

THE CITY MADAM

To the truly Noble and Virtuous
Lady Ann, Countess of Oxford.

Honored Lady!
In that age when wit and learning were not conquered by
injury and violence, this poem was the object of love and   5
commendations, it being composed by an infallible pen,
and censured by an unerring auditory. In this epistle I
shall not need to make an apology for plays in general by
exhibiting their antiquity and utility: in a word, they are
mirrors or glasses which none but deformed faces, and   10
fouler consciences fear to look into. The encouragement I
had to prefer this dedication to your powerful protection
proceeds from the universal fame of the deceased author,
who (although he composed many) writ none amiss, and
this may justly be ranked among his best. I have redeemed   15
it from the teeth of time, by committing of it to the press, but
more in imploring your patronage. I will not slander it with
my praises, it is commendations enough to call it Massinger's. If it may gain your allowance and pardon, I am
highly gratified, and desire only to wear the happy title of,   20
     Madam,
      Your Humblest Servant,
       Andrew Pennycuicke.

1–2. To the . . . / . . . Oxford. *For*
the variant dedications, see Introduction,
p. xx.

3. Lady!] Sir! *in copies dedicated to*
Wrath, Freake, Steadwell, and Lee.
21. Madam,] Sir, *in copies dedicated*
to Wrath, Freake, Steadwell, and Lee.

2. *Ann, Countess of Oxford*] daughter of Paul, second Viscount Bayning,
and of Diana his wife; married Aubrey DeVere, the twentieth and last
Earl of Oxford, but died soon after her marriage, and was buried in St.
John Baptist's Chapel, Westminster Abbey, September 27, 1659 (Kirk,
p. 15).

23. *Andrew Pennycuicke*] born October 1, 1620. As an actor, he was
presumably connected with Queen Henrietta's Company or Beeston's
Boys (Bentley, II, 524–525).

The Actors' Names

LORD LACY
SIR JOHN FRUGAL, *a merchant*
SIR MAURICE LACY, *son to Lord Lacy*
MR. PLENTY, *a country gentleman*
LUKE, *brother to Sir John Frugal*   5
OLD GOLDWIRE ⎫
OLD TRADEWELL ⎭ *two gentlemen*
YOUNG GOLDWIRE ⎫
YOUNG TRADEWELL ⎭ *their sons, prentices to Sir John Frugal*   10
STARGAZE, *an astrologer*
FORTUNE, *a decayed merchant*
HOYST, *a decayed gentleman*
PENURY   15
HOLDFAST, *a steward*
RAMBLE ⎫
SCUFFLE ⎭ *two hectors*
DING'EM, *a pimp*   20
GETTALL, *a box-keeper*
LADY FRUGAL
ANNE ⎫
MARY ⎭ *her daughters*   25
MILLISCENT, *her woman*
SHAVE'EM, *a wench*
SECRET, *a bawd*
[PAGE TO SIR MAURICE LACY
SHERIFF, MARSHALL, SERGEANTS, SERVINGMEN, MUSICIANS   30
CERBERUS, CHARON, ORPHEUS, CHORUS]

Scene, *London*

2, 5, 10. Sir John Frugal] *Gifford;*   John Lacy Q.
Sir John Rich Q.   22. Lady Frugal] *Gifford;* Lady
3. Sir Maurice Lacy] *Dodsley;* Sir   Rich Q.

18. *hectors*] bullies.
21. *box-keeper*] "the keeper of the dice and box at a gaming table" (*OED*).

-4-

The City Madam

[I.i]   *Enter* [Young] Goldwire *and* [Young] Tradewell.

YOUNG GOLDWIRE.
    The ship is safe in the Pool then?
YOUNG TRADEWELL.   And makes good,
    In her rich fraught, the name she bears, the *Speedwell:*
    My master will find it, for on my certain knowledge
    For every hundred that he ventured in her
    She hath return'd him five.
YOUNG GOLDWIRE.   And it comes timely,   5
    For besides a payment on the nail for a manor
    Late purchas'd by my master, his young daughters
    Are ripe for marriage.
YOUNG TRADEWELL.   Who? Nan and Mall?
YOUNG GOLDWIRE.
    Mistress Anne and Mary, and with some addition,
    Or 'tis more punishable in our house   10
    Than *scandalum magnatum.*
YOUNG TRADEWELL.   'Tis great pity
    Such a gentleman as my master (for that title
    His being a citizen cannot take from him)
    Hath no male heir to inherit his estate,
    And keep his name alive.
YOUNG GOLDWIRE.   The want of one   15
    Swells my young mistresses, and their madam mother,
    With hopes above their birth and scale. Their dreams are
    Of being made countesses, and they take state

---

    1. *the Pool*] the part of the River Thames between London Bridge and
Limehouse Point.
    2. *fraught*] freight.
    6. *on the nail*] on the spot; at once.
    9. *addition*] added term of respect.
    11. *scandalum magnatum*] "The utterance or punishment of a malicious
report against any person holding a position of dignity" (*OED*).

As they were such already. When you went
To the Indies, there was some shape and proportion   20
Of a merchant's house in our family; but since
My master, to gain precedency for my mistress
Above some elder merchants' wives, was knighted,
'Tis grown a little court in bravery,
Variety of fashions, and those rich ones: 25
There are few great ladies going to a masque
That do outshine ours in their everyday habits.

YOUNG TRADEWELL.

'Tis strange my master in his wisdom can
Give the reins to such exorbitancy.

YOUNG GOLDWIRE.   He must,
Or there's no peace nor rest for him at home;   30
I grant his state will bear it, yet he's censur'd
For his indulgence, and for Sir John Frugal,
By some styl'd Sir John Prodigal.

YOUNG TRADEWELL.   Is his brother,
Master Luke Frugal, living?

YOUNG GOLDWIRE.   Yes, the more
His misery, poor man.

YOUNG TRADEWELL.   Still in the Counter?   35

YOUNG GOLDWIRE.

In a worser place. He was redeemed from the hole,
To live in our house in hell: since, his base usage
Consider'd, 'tis no better. My proud lady
Admits him to her table; marry, ever
Beneath the salt, and there he sits the subject   40

---

24. *bravery*] splendor.   27. *habits*] clothes.

35. *the Counter*] the name of two debtors' prisons in London in the seventeenth century, one in the Poultry, the other in Wood Street. It was in the latter, to judge from the reference to "the hole" in the following line, that Luke was imprisoned.

36. *the hole*] "one of the wretched departments of a gaol, in which prisoners, who could not afford to pay for better accommodations, were obliged to take up their residence" (Gifford). He notes that *hell* (line 37) "was a spot yet more wretched than the *hole*," and quotes from *The Counter-rat* (1658) the line: "In Wood-street's *hole*, or Poultry's *hell*."

40. *Beneath the salt*] the salt was placed near the middle of the table; persons of inferior station were seated below it, persons of distinction above it.

Of her contempt and scorn; and dinner ended,
His courteous nieces find employment for him
Fitting an under-prentice, or a footman,
And not an uncle.

YOUNG TRADEWELL.   I wonder, being a scholar
Well read, and travel'd, the world yielding means   45
For men of such desert, he should endure it.

YOUNG GOLDWIRE.
He does, with a strange patience; and to us
The servants so familiar, nay humble.

Enter Stargaze, Lady [Frugal], Anne, Mary, Milliscent, *in several
postures, with looking glasses at their girdles.*

I'll tell you—but I am cut off. Look these
Like a citizen's wife and daughters?

YOUNG TRADEWELL.   In their habits   50
They appear other things; but what are the motives
Of this strange preparation?

YOUNG GOLDWIRE.   The young wagtails
Expect their suitors: the first, the son and heir
Of the Lord Lacy, who needs my master's money,
As his daughter does his honor; the second, Master Plenty,   55
A roughhewn gentleman, and newly come
To a great estate; and so all aids of art
In them's excusable.

LADY FRUGAL.   You have done your parts here:
To your study, and be curious in the search
Of the nativities.   *Exit* Stargaze.

YOUNG TRADEWELL.   Methinks the mother,   60
As if she could renew her youth, in care,
Nay, curiosity to appear lovely,
Comes not behind her daughters.

YOUNG GOLDWIRE.   Keeps the first place,
And though the church-book speak her fifty, they

48.1–2. *Enter   Stargaze . . . girdles.*]
after l. 46 Q.

59–60. *curious . . . nativities*] careful in casting the horoscopes.
62. *curiosity*] undue fastidiousness.

−7−

That say she can write thirty, more offend her, 65
Than if they tax'd her honesty: t'other day
A tenant of hers, instructed in her humor,
But one she never saw, being brought before her,
For saying only, "Good young mistress, help me
To the speech of your lady mother," so far pleas'd her, 70
That he got his lease renew'd for't.

YOUNG TRADEWELL.   How she bristles!
Prithee, observe her.

MILLISCENT.   As I hope to see
A country knight's son and heir walk bare before you
When you are a countess, as you may be one
When my master dies, or leaves trading; and I continuing 75
Your principal woman, take the upper hand
Of a squire's wife, though a justice, as I must
By the place you give me, you look now as young
As when you were married.

LADY FRUGAL.   I think I bear my years well.

MILLISCENT.
Why should you talk of years? Time hath not plow'd 80
One furrow in your face; and were you not known
The mother of my young ladies, you might pass
For a virgin of fifteen.

YOUNG TRADEWELL.   Here's no gross flattery!
Will she swallow this?

YOUNG GOLDWIRE.   You see she does, and glibly.

MILLISCENT.
You never can be old; wear but a mask 85
Forty years hence, and you will still seem young
In your other parts. What a waist is here! O Venus!
That I had been born a King! and here a hand
To be kiss'd ever—pardon my boldness, madam—
Then, for a leg and foot, you will be courted 90
When a great grandmother.

---

67. *humor*] disposition, temperament.

73. *walk . . . you*] walk with his hat off in your presence (as a mark of respect).

76. *take . . . hand*] take precedence.

77. *though a justice*] though the squire (whose wife Milliscent hopes to take precedence over) be a judicial officer.

LADY FRUGAL.   These indeed, wench, are not
So subject to decayings as the face;
Their comeliness lasts longer.
MILLISCENT.   Ever, ever!
Such a rare featur'd and proportion'd madam
London could never boast of.
LADY FRUGAL.   Where are my shoes?   95
MILLISCENT.
Those that your ladyship gave order should
Be made of the Spanish perfum'd skins?
LADY FRUGAL.   The same.
MILLISCENT.
I sent the prison-bird this morning for 'em,
But he neglects his duty.
ANNE.   He is grown
Exceeding careless.
MARY.   And begins to murmur   100
At our commands, and sometimes grumbles to us,
He is forsooth our uncle!
LADY FRUGAL.   He is your slave,
And as such use him.
ANNE.   Willingly, but he's grown
Rebellious, madam.
YOUNG GOLDWIRE.   Nay, like hen, like chicken.
LADY FRUGAL.
I'll humble him.

Enter Luke, *with shoes, garters and roses.*

YOUNG GOLDWIRE.   Here he comes sweating all over;   105
He shows like a walking frippery.
LADY FRUGAL.   Very good, sir:
Were you drunk last night, that you could rise no sooner
With humble diligence to do what my daughters
And woman did command you.

105. S.D.] *after* madam (*l. 104*) *Q*.

---

105. S.D. *roses*] "knots of ribands to be fixed on the shoes" (Gifford).
106. *shows*] looks.
106. *frippery*] an old-clothes shop.

LUKE.   Drunk, an't please you?

LADY FRUGAL.

 Drunk, I said, sirrah! Dar'st thou in a look   110
 Repine, or grumble? Thou unthankful wretch,
 Did our charity redeem thee out of prison,
 (Thy patrimony spent), ragged and lousy,
 When the sheriff's basket, and his broken meat,
 Were your festival-exceedings, and is this   115
 So soon forgotten?

LUKE.   I confess I am
 Your creature, madam.

LADY FRUGAL.   And good reason why
 You should continue so.

ANNE.   Who did new clothe you?

MARY.

 Admitted you to the dining room?

MILLISCENT.   Allowed you
 A fresh bed in the garret?

LADY FRUGAL.   Or from whom   120
 Receiv'd you spending money?

LUKE.   I owe all this
 To your goodness, madam; for it you have my prayers,
 The beggar's satisfaction; all my studies
 (Forgetting what I was, but with all duty
 Rememb'ring what I am) are how to please you.   125
 And if in my long stay I have offended,
 I ask your pardon. Though you may consider,
 Being forc'd to fetch these from the Old Exchange,
 These from the Tower, and these from Westminster,
 I could not come much sooner.

YOUNG GOLDWIRE.   Here was a walk   130

---

109. *an't*] if it.

114. *sheriff's basket*] "It was customary formerly to send the relicks of the sheriff's table in baskets, to the poor confined in the prisons" (Nares).

115. *festival-exceedings*] "college slang for extra commons allowed on festival occasions" (Kirk).

123. *studies*] endeavors.

128. *Old Exchange*] Built by Sir Thomas Gresham in 1566–1567; named the Royal Exchange after a visit from Queen Elizabeth in 1570; and often termed the Old Exchange after a second Exchange was built in 1609.

To breathe a footman!

ANNE.   'Tis a curious fan.

MARY.

These roses will show rare; would 'twere in fashion
That the garters might be seen too.

MILLISCENT.   Many ladies
That know they have good legs, wish the same with you:
Men that way have th' advantage.

LUKE [*aside to* Young Goldwire].   I was with   135
The lady, and delivered her the satin
For her gown, and velvet for her petticoat;
This night she vows she'll pay you.

YOUNG GOLDWIRE.   How I am bound
To your favor, Master Luke!

MILLISCENT.   As I live, you will
Perfume all rooms you walk in.

LADY FRUGAL.   Get your fur,   140
You shall pull 'em on within.

YOUNG GOLDWIRE.   That servile office   *Exit* Luke.
Her pride imposes on him.

SIR JOHN (*within*).   Goldwire! Tradewell!

YOUNG TRADEWELL.

My master calls. —We come, sir.
                    Exeunt [Young] Goldwire, [Young] Tradewell.

                    Enter Holdfast *with porters.*

LADY FRUGAL.   What have you brought there?

HOLDFAST.

The cream of the market, provision enough
To serve a garrison. I weep to think on't.   145
When my master got his wealth, his family fed
On roots and livers, and necks of beef on Sundays.
But now I fear it will be spent in poultry.
Butcher's meat will not go down.

LADY FRUGAL.   Why, you rascal, is it
At your expense? What cooks have you provided?   150

---

131. *breathe*] exercise.
140. *fur*] "a piece of undressed skin . . . used . . . in lieu of a shoeing
horn" (Gifford).

HOLDFAST.

    The best of the city. They have wrought at my lord mayor's.

ANNE.

    Fie on 'em! they smell of Fleet-lane and Pie-corner.

MARY.

    And thinks the happiness of man's life consists
    In a mighty shoulder of mutton.

LADY FRUGAL.   I'll have none

    Shall touch what I shall eat, you grumbling cur,   155
    But Frenchmen and Italians; they wear satin,
    And dish no meat but in silver.

HOLDFAST.   You may want, though,

    A dish or two when the service ends.

LADY FRUGAL.   Leave prating,

    I'll have my will; do you as I command you.   *Exeunt.*

    [I.ii]   *Enter* [Sir Maurice] Lacy *and* Page.

SIR MAURICE.

    You were with Plenty?

PAGE.   Yes, sir.

SIR MAURICE.   And what answer

    Return'd the clown?

PAGE.   Clown sir! he is transform'd,

    And grown a gallant of the last edition;
    More rich than gaudy in his habit; yet
    The freedom and the bluntness of his language   5
    Continues with him. When I told him that
    You gave him caution, as he lov'd the peace
    And safety of his life, he should forbear
    To pass the merchant's threshold, until you,
    Of his two daughters, had made choice of her   10
    Whom you design'd to honor as your wife,
    He smil'd in scorn.

SIR MAURICE.   In scorn?

PAGE.   His words confirm'd it.

---

    152. *Fleet-lane and Pie-corner*] where a number of cooks' shops were located.
    157. *want*] lack.
[I.ii]
    3. *the last edition*] the latest fashion.

They were few, but to this purpose: "Tell your master,
Though his lordship in reversion were now his,
It cannot awe me. I was born a free man,   15
And will not yield in the way of affection
Precedence to him. I will visit 'em,
Though he sat porter to deny my entrance.
When I meet him next, I'll say more to his face.
Deliver thou this"—then gave me a piece   20
To help my memory, and so we parted.

SIR MAURICE.
Where got he this spirit?

PAGE.   At the academy of valor,
Newly erected for the institution
Of elder brothers, where they are taught the ways,
Though they refuse to seal for a duelist,   25
How to decline a challenge. He himself
Can best resolve you.

Enter Plenty *and three serving-men.*

SIR MAURICE.   You, sir!

PLENTY.   What with me, sir!
How big you look! I will not loose a hat
To a hair's breadth. Move your beaver, I'll move mine,
Or if you desire to prove your sword, mine hangs   30
As near my right hand, and will as soon out,
Though I keep not a fencer to breathe me.
Walk into Moorfields—I dare look on your Toledo.

---

14. *Though . . . his*] though he had already succeeded to the title which
he will inherit upon his father's death.

16. *in . . . affection*] in the matter of love.

20. *a piece*] a piece of money, given to the Page as a tip.

22. *academy of valor*] a school furnishing instruction in fencing, and in
points of honor.

24–26. *taught . . . challenge*] taught how, without engaging in a duel, to
decline a challenge, and yet preserve the semblance of honor.

28–29. *I . . . breadth*] I will not remove my hat (in deference to you) by a
hair's breadth.

29. *beaver*] hat made of beaver's fur.   32. *breathe*] exercise.

33. *Moorfields*] a piece of ground north of the old city wall of London
where duels were often fought.

33. *Toledo*] a Spanish sword or sword-blade, made at Toledo.

Do not show a foolish valor in the streets,
To make work for shopkeepers and their clubs;   35
'Tis scurvy, and the women will laugh at us.

SIR MAURICE.
You presume on the protection of your hinds.

PLENTY.
I scorn it:
Though I keep men, I fight not with their fingers,
Nor make it my religion to follow   40
The gallant's fashion, to have my family
Consisting in a footman and a page,
And those two sometimes hungry. I can feed these,
And clothe 'em too, my gay sir.

SIR MAURICE.   What a fine man
Hath your tailor made you!

PLENTY.   'Tis quite contrary,   45
I have made my tailor, for my clothes are paid for
As soon as put on, a sin your man of title
Is seldom guilty of, but heaven forgive it.
I have other faults, too, very incident
To a plain gentleman. I eat my venison   50
With my neighbors in the country, and present not
My pheasants, partridges, and grouse to the usurer,
Nor ever yet paid brokage to his scrivener.
I flatter not my mercer's wife, nor feast her
With the first cherries, or peascods, to prepare me   55
Credit with her husband, when I come to London.
The wool of my sheep, or a score or two of fat oxen
In Smithfield, give me money for my expenses.
I can make my wife a jointure of such lands too
As are not encumber'd, no annuity   60

---

37. *hinds*] farm servants, with reference to the three serving-men who
have entered with Plenty at 1.27.

53. *paid brokage*] bribed.   53. *scrivener*] scribe, clerk.

54. *mercer*] "A dealer in textile fabrics, especially silks and other costly
materials" (*OED*).

58. *Smithfield*] ". . . for centuries, and until 1855, used as a market for
sheep, horses, cattle, and hay. It is sometimes called *West Smithfield*, to
distinguish it from a place of smaller consequence of the same name in the
east of London" (Wheatley).

Or statute lying on 'em. This I can do,
And it please your future honor, and why therefore
You should forbid my being a suitor with you
My dullness apprehends not.

PAGE.   This is bitter.

SIR MAURICE.
I have heard you, sir, and in my patience shown   65
Too much of the stoic's. But to parley further,
Or answer your gross jeers, would write me coward.
This only: thy great grandfather was a butcher,
And his son a grazier; thy sire, constable
Of the hundred, and thou the first of your dunghill   70
Created gentleman. Now you may come on, sir,
You, and your thrashers.

PLENTY [*to his Serving-men*].   Stir not on your lives.—
This for the grazier, this for the butcher.   *They fight.*

SIR MAURICE.   So, sir!

PAGE.
I'll not stand idle. —[*To the Serving-men.*] Draw! My little
    rapier
Against your bumb blades. I'll one by one despatch you,   75
Then house this instrument of death and horror.

Enter Sir John [Frugal], Luke, [Young] Goldwire, [Young]
Tradewell.

SIR JOHN.
Beat down their weapons. My gate ruffians' hall!
What insolence is this?

LUKE.   Noble Sir Maurice,
Worshipful Master Plenty—

SIR JOHN.   I blush for you.
Men of your quality expose your fame   80

---

61. statute] *Dodsley;* statue *Q.*   73. grazier] *Dodsley;* grasiers *Q.*

---

69. *grazier*] "one who feeds cattle for the market" (*OED*).
70. *hundred*] "A subdivision of a county or shire, having its own court"
(*OED*).
75. *bumb blades*] large swords.
77. *ruffians' hall*] "An allusion to Ruffian Hall in West Smithfield where
duels were commonly fought" (Kirk).
80. *fame*] reputation.

To every vulgar censure! This at midnight
After a drunken supper in a tavern,
(No civil man abroad to censure it)
Had shown poor in you, but in the day, and view
Of all that pass by, monstrous!

PLENTY.   Very well, sir;   85
You look'd for this defense.

SIR MAURICE.   'Tis thy protection,
But it will deceive thee.

SIR JOHN.   Hold! If you proceed thus
I must make use of the next justice's power,
And leave persuasion, and in plain terms tell you

            Enter Lady [Frugal], Anne, Mary, *and* Milliscent.

Neither your birth, Sir Maurice, nor [*to* Plenty] your
    wealth,   90
Shall privilege this riot. See whom you have drawn
To be spectators of it? Can you imagine
It can stand with the credit of my daughters,
To be the argument of your swords? i' th' street too?
Nay, ere you do salute, or I give way   95
To any private conference, shake hands
In sign of peace. He that draws back, parts with
My good opinion. [*They shake hands.*] This is as it should be.
Make your approaches, and if their affection
Can sympathize with yours, they shall not come,   100
On my credit, beggars to you. I will hear
What you reply within.

SIR MAURICE [*to* Anne].   May I have the honor
To support you, lady?

PLENTY [*to* Mary].   I know not what's supporting,
But by this fair hand, glove and all, I love you.
                            Exeunt omnes praeter Luke.

86. look'd] *Mason;* look *Q.*

---

95. *salute*] make your addresses (to the women).
101. *credit*] faith.
104.1. *praeter*] except.

To him enter Hoyst, Penury, Fortune.

LUKE.

You are come with all advantage. I will help you   105
To the speech of my brother.

FORTUNE.   Have you mov'd him for us?

LUKE.

With the best of my endeavors, and I hope
You'll find him tractable.

PENURY.   Heaven grant he prove so.

HOYST.

Howe'er, I'll speak my mind.

Enter Lord Lacy.

LUKE.   Do so, Master Hoyst.

Go in. I'll pay my duty to this lord,   110
And then I am wholly yours.

                        [*Exeunt* Hoyst, Penury, Fortune.]
                        —Heaven bless your honor.

LORD LACY.

Your hand, Master Luke. The world's much chang'd with you
Within these few months; then you were the gallant:
No meeting at the horse race, cocking, hunting,
Shooting, or bowling, at which Master Luke   115
Was not a principal gamester, and companion
For the nobility.

LUKE.   I have paid dear

For those follies, my good lord; and 'tis but justice
That such as soar above their pitch, and will not
Be warn'd by my example, should like me   120
Share in the miseries that wait upon't.
Your honor in your charity may do well
Not to upbraid me with those weaknesses
Too late repented.

LORD LACY.   I nor do, nor will;

And you shall find I'll lend a helping hand   125
To raise your fortunes. How deals your brother with you?

LUKE.

Beyond my merit, I thank his goodness for't.

---

106. *mov'd . . . us*] appealed to him in our behalf.

−17−

I am a free man, all my debts discharg'd,
Nor does one creditor undone by me
Curse my loose riots. I have meat and clothes,   130
Time to ask heaven remission for what's past;
Cares of the world by me are laid aside,
My present poverty's a blessing to me;
And though I have been long, I dare not say
I ever liv'd till now.

LORD LACY.   You bear it well;   135
Yet as you wish I should receive for truth
What you deliver, with that truth acquaint me
With your brother's inclination. I have heard
In the acquisition of his wealth, he weighs not
Whose ruins he builds upon.

LUKE.   In that, report   140
Wrongs him, my lord. He is a citizen,
And would increase his heap, and will not lose
Where the law gives him. Such as are wordly wise
Pursue that track, or they will ne'er wear scarlet.
But if your honor please to know his temper,   145
You are come opportunely. I can bring you
Where you unseen shall see and hear his carriage
Towards some poor men, whose making or undoing
Depend upon his pleasure.

LORD LACY.   To my wish:
I know no object that could more content me.   *Exeunt.* 150

[I.iii]
Enter Sir John [Frugal], Hoyst, Fortune, Penury, [Young] Goldwire.

SIR JOHN.
What would you have me do?—reach me a chair.
When I lent my moneys I appear'd an angel;
But now I would call in mine own, a devil.

---

144. track] *Gifford;* tract *Q.*   *"A Table,/ Count Book,/ Standish,/*
144–148.] *Q contains marginal S.D.*   *Chair and/ stools set out."*

---

144. *wear scarlet*] become aldermen, sheriffs, lord mayors, or other city officials.
147. *carriage*] behavior.

−18−

HOYST.

    Were you the devil's dam, you must stay till I have it,

    For as I am a gentleman—

Enter Luke, *placing the* Lord Lacy.

LUKE.   There you may hear all.   5

HOYST.

    I pawn'd you my land for the tenth part of the value.

    Now, 'cause I am a gamester, and keep ordinaries,

    And a livery punk or so, and trade not with

    The money-mongers' wives, not one will be bound for me.

    'Tis a hard case; you must give me longer day   10

    Or I shall grow very angry.

SIR JOHN.   Fret, and spare not.

    I know no obligation lies upon me

    With my honey to feed drones. But to the purpose:

    How much owes Penury?

YOUNG GOLDWIRE.   Two hundred pounds:

    His bond three times since forfeited.

SIR JOHN.   Is it su'd?   15

YOUNG GOLDWIRE.

    Yes, sir, and execution out against him.

SIR JOHN.

    For body and goods?

YOUNG GOLDWIRE.   For both, sir.

SIR JOHN.   See it serv'd.

PENURY.

    I am undone; my wife and family

    Must starve for want of bread.

SIR JOHN.   More infidel thou,

    In not providing better to support 'em.   20

---

    5. S.D. *placing*] i.e., stationing the Lord Lacy in a position where he can witness the scene that follows and comment on it (as at lines 73–74, 96–97), while remaining concealed from the others on stage until he comes forward at line 121.

    7. *ordinaries*] eating houses or taverns where meals were provided at a fixed price.

    8. *livery*] kept at livery, or for hire.

    8. *punk*] prostitute.

    10. *longer day*] more time.

What's Fortune's debt?

YOUNG GOLDWIRE.   A thousand, sir.

SIR JOHN.   An estate
For a good man! You were the glorious trader,
Embrac'd all bargains; the main venturer
In every ship that launch'd forth; kept your wife
As a lady; she had her coach, her choice   25
Of summer-houses, built with other men's moneys
Took up at interest, the certain road
To Ludgate in a citizen. Pray you acquaint me,
How were my thousand pounds employ'd?

FORTUNE.   Insult not
On my calamity, though being a debtor,   30
And a slave to him that lends, I must endure it.
You hear me speak thus much in my defense;
Losses at sea, and those, sir, great and many,
By storms and tempests, not domestical riots
In soothing my wife's humor, or mine own,   35
Have brought me to this low ebb.

SIR JOHN.   Suppose this true,
What is't to me? I must and will have my money,
Or I'll protest you first, and that done have
The statute made for bankrupts serv'd upon you.

FORTUNE.
'Tis in your power, but not in mine to shun it.   40

LUKE [comes forward].
Not as a brother, sir, but with such duty
As I should use unto my father, since
Your charity is my parent, give me leave
To speak my thoughts.

SIR JOHN.   What would you say?

LUKE.   No word, sir,
I hope shall give offense; nor let it relish   45
Of flattery, though I proclaim aloud:
I glory in the bravery of your mind,
To which your wealth's a servant. Not that riches

---

28. *Ludgate*] a prison for debtors and bankrupts.
38. *protest*] "To make a formal written declaration of the non-acceptance
or non-payment of (a bill of exchange) when duly presented" (*OED*).

Is or should be contemn'd, it being a blessing
Deriv'd from heaven, and by your industry   50
Pull'd down upon you; but in this, dear sir,
You have many equals: such a man's possessions
Extend as far as yours, a second hath
His bags as full; a third in credit flies
As high in the popular voice: but the distinction   55
And noble difference by which you are
Divided from 'em, is that you are styl'd
Gentle in your abundance, good in plenty,
And that you feel compassion in your bowels
Of others' miseries (I have found it, sir,   60
Heaven keep me thankful for't), while they are curs'd
As rigid and inexorable.

SIR JOHN.   I delight not
To hear this spoke to my face.

LUKE.   That shall not grieve you.
Your affability and mildness, cloth'd
In the garments of your debtors' breath,   65
Shall everywhere, though you strive to conceal it,
Be seen and wonder'd at, and in the act
With a prodigal hand rewarded. Whereas such
As are born only for themselves, and live so,
Though prosperous in worldly understandings,   70
Are but like beasts of rapine, that by odds
Of strength, usurp and tyrannize o'er others
Brought under their subjection.

LORD LACY.   A rare fellow!
I am strangely taken with him.

LUKE.   Can you think, sir,
In your unquestion'd wisdom, I beseech you,   75
The goods of this poor man sold at an outcry,
His wife turn'd out of doors, his children forc'd
To beg their bread: this gentleman's estate,
By wrong extorted, can advantage you?

HOYST.
If it thrive with him, hang me, as it will damn him   80
If he be not converted.

---

76. *at an outcry*] at a public auction.

LUKE.   You are too violent.—
Or that the ruin of this once brave merchant
(For such he was esteem'd, though now decay'd)
Will raise your reputation with good men?
But you may urge—pray you pardon me, my zeal   85
Makes me thus bold and vehement—in this
You satisfy your anger and revenge
For being defeated. Suppose this, it will not
Repair your loss, and there was never yet
But shame and scandal in a victory,   90
When the rebels unto reason, passions, fought it.
Then for revenge, by great souls it was ever
Contemn'd, though offered; entertain'd by none
But cowards, base and abject spirits, strangers
To moral honesty, and never yet   95
Acquainted with religion.
LORD LACY.   Our divines
Cannot speak more effectually.
SIR JOHN.   Shall I be
Talk'd out of my money?
LUKE.   No, sir, but entreated
To do yourself a benefit, and preserve
What you possess entire.
SIR JOHN.   How, my good brother?   100
LUKE.
By making these your beadsmen. When they eat,
Their thanks, next heaven, will be paid to your mercy;
When your ships are at sea, their prayers will swell
The sails with prosperous winds, and guard 'em from
Tempests and pirates: keep your warehouses   105
From fire, or quench 'em with their tears—
SIR JOHN.   No more.
LUKE.
—Write you a good man in the people's hearts,
Follow you everywhere.

91. reason] *Dodsley;* reasons *Q.*

---

101. *beadsmen*] "such as are engaged, in consequence of past or present favours, to pray for their benefactors" (Gifford).
    102. *next*] after.

SIR JOHN.   If this could be—

LUKE.

It must, or our devotions are but words.
I see a gentle promise in your eye,   110
Make it a blessed act, and poor me rich
In being the instrument.

SIR JOHN.   You shall prevail.
Give 'em longer day. But do you hear, no talk of't.
Should this arrive at twelve on the Exchange,
I shall be laugh'd at for my foolish pity,   115
Which money men hate deadly. Take your own time,
But see you break not. Carry 'em to the cellar,
Drink a health, and thank your orator.

PENURY.   On our knees, sir.

FORTUNE.

Honest Master Luke!

HOYST.   I bless the Counter where
You learn'd this rhetoric.

LUKE.   No more of that, friends.   120

Exeunt Luke, Hoyst, Fortune, Penury.

[Lord Lacy *comes forward.*]

SIR JOHN.

My honorable lord.

LORD LACY.   I have seen and heard all—
Excuse my manners—and wish heartily
You were all of a piece. Your charity to your debtors,
I do commend, but where you should express
Your piety to the height, I must boldly tell you   125
You show yourself an atheist.

SIR JOHN.   Make me know
My error, and for what I am thus censur'd,
And I will purge myself, or else confess
A guilty cause.

LORD LACY.   It is your harsh demeanor
To your poor brother.

SIR JOHN.   Is that all?

LORD LACY.   'Tis more   130

---

117. *break not*] do not fail to meet your obligation at the appointed time.

Than can admit defense. You keep him as
A parasite to your table, subject to
The scorn of your proud wife, an underling
To his own nieces. And can I with mine honor
Mix my blood with his, that is not sensible   135
Of his brother's miseries?

SIR JOHN.   Pray you, take me with you,
And let me yield my reasons why I am
No opener handed to him. I was born
His elder brother, yet my father's fondness
To him, the younger, robb'd me of my birthright: 140
He had a fair estate, which his loose riots
Soon brought to nothing. Wants grew heavy on him,
And when laid up for debt, of all forsaken,
And in his own hopes lost, I did redeem him.

LORD LACY.
You could not do less.

SIR JOHN.   Was I bound to it, my lord?   145
What I possess, I may with justice call
The harvest of my industry. Would you have me,
Neglecting mine own family, to give up
My estate to his disposure?

LORD LACY.   I would have you,
What's pass'd forgot, to use him as a brother;   150
A brother of fair parts, of a clear soul,
Religious, good, and honest.

SIR JOHN.   Outward gloss
Often deceives; may it not prove so in him!
And yet my long acquaintance with his nature
Renders me doubtful; but that shall not make   155
A breach between us. Let us in to dinner,
And what trust, or employment you think fit
Shall be conferred upon him. If he prove
True gold in the touch, I'll be no mourner for it.

131. him as] *Q* (*corrected*); Hymas
Q (*uncorrected*).

---

136. *take me with you*] hear me out.
159. *in the touch*] when put to the test (the quality of gold or silver was
tested by rubbing it upon a touchstone).

LORD LACY.
   If counterfeit, I'll never trust my judgment.   *Exeunt.* 160

[II.i]
   Enter Luke, Holdfast, [Young] Goldwire, [Young] Tradewell.

HOLDFAST.
   The like was never seen.
LUKE.   Why in this rage, man?
HOLDFAST.
   Men may talk of country Christmasses, and court gluttony,
   Their thirty-pound butter'd eggs, their pies of carps' tongues,
   Their pheasants drench'd with ambergris, the carcases
   Of three fat wethers bruised for gravy to   5
   Make sauce for a single peacock, yet their feasts
   Were fasts compar'd with the city's.
YOUNG TRADEWELL.   What dear dainty
   Was it thou murmur'st at?
HOLDFAST.   Did you not observe it?
   There were three sucking pigs serv'd up in a dish,
   Took from the sow as soon as farrowed,   10
   A fortnight fed with dates, and muscadine,
   That stood my master in twenty marks apiece,
   Besides the puddings in their bellies made
   Of I know not what. I dare swear the cook that dress'd it
   Was the devil disguis'd like a Dutchman.
YOUNG GOLDWIRE.   Yet all this   15
   Will not make you fat, fellow Holdfast.
HOLDFAST.   I am rather
   Starv'd to look on't. But here's the mischief—though
   The dishes were rais'd one upon another
   As woodmongers do billets, for the first,
   The second, and third course, and most of the shops   20
   Of the best confectioners in London ransack'd

---

4. *ambergris*] "Literally grey amber, from its colour and perfume . . . .
It is found floating on the sea in warm climates, and is now generally
agreed by chemists to be produced in the stomach of the . . . spermaceti
whale" (Nares).
   7. *dear*] expensive.
   11. *muscadine*] "A rich sort of wine" (Nares).

-25-

To furnish out a banquet, yet my lady
Call'd me penurious rascal, and cried out,
There was nothing worth the eating.

YOUNG GOLDWIRE.   You must have patience,
This is not done often.

HOLDFAST.   'Tis not fit it should;   25
Three such dinners more would break an alderman,
And make him give up his cloak. I am resolv'd
To have no hand in't. I'll make up my accompts,
And since my master longs to be undone,
The great fiend be his steward; I will pray   30
And bless my self from him.   *Exit* Holdfast.

YOUNG GOLDWIRE.   The wretch shows in this
An honest care.

LUKE.   Out on him! With the fortune
Of a slave, he has the mind of one. However
She bears me hard, I like my lady's humor,
And my brother's suffrage to it. They are now   35
Busy on all hands; one side eager for
Large portions, the other arguing strictly
For jointures and security; but this
Being above our scale, no way concerns us.
How dull you look! In the meantime how intend you   40
To spend the hours?

YOUNG GOLDWIRE.   We well know how we would,
But dare not serve your wills.

YOUNG TRADEWELL.   Being prentices,
We are bound to attendance.

LUKE.   Have you almost serv'd out
The term of your indentures, yet make conscience
By starts to use your liberty? [*To* Young Tradewell.]
                    Hast thou traded   45
In the other world, expos'd unto all dangers,
To make thy master rich, yet dar'st not take

---

22. *a banquet*] "A course of sweetmeats, fruit, and wine; a dessert" (*OED*).
28. *accompts*] accounts.
44. *indentures*] "The contract by which an apprentice is bound to the master who undertakes to teach him a trade" (*OED*).
44–45. *make . . . liberty*] are scrupulous about using the freedom of your position from time to time.

Some portion of the profit for thy pleasure?
[*To* Young Goldwire.] Or wilt thou, being keeper of the cash,
Like an ass that carries dainties, feed on thistles?   50
Are you gentlemen born, yet have no gallant tincture
Of gentry in you? You are no mechanics,
Nor serve some needy shopkeeper, who surveys
His everyday takings. You have in your keeping
A mass of wealth, from which you may take boldly,   55
And no way be discover'd. He's no rich man
That knows all he possesses, and leaves nothing
For his servants to make prey of. I blush for you,
Blush at your poverty of spirit, you
The brave sparks of the city!

YOUNG GOLDWIRE.   Master Luke,   60
I wonder you should urge this, having felt
What misery follows riot.

YOUNG TRADEWELL.   And the penance
You endur'd for't in the Counter.

LUKE.   You are fools,
The case is not the same. I spent mine own money,
And my stock being small, no marvel 'twas soon wasted.   65
But you without the least doubt or suspicion,
If cautelous, may make bold with your master's.
As for example: when his ships come home,
And you take your receipts, as 'tis the fashion,
For fifty bales of silk you may write forty;   70
Or for so many pieces of cloth of bodkin,
Tissue, gold, silver, velvets, satins, taffetas,
A piece of each deducted from the gross
Will never be miss'd; a dash of a pen will do it.

YOUNG TRADEWELL.
Aye, but our fathers' bonds that lie in pawn   75
For our honesties must pay for't.

LUKE.   A mere bugbear
Invented to fright children! As I live,
Were I the master of my brother's fortunes,
I should glory in such servants. Did'st thou know

---

52. *mechanics*] manual laborers.
67. *cautelous*] crafty, cautious.

What ravishing lechery it is to enter   80
An ordinary, cap-a-pe, trimm'd like a gallant,
(For which in trunks conceal'd be ever furnish'd),
The reverence, respect, the crouches, cringes
The musical chime of gold in your cramm'd pockets
Commands from the attendants, and poor porters—   85

YOUNG TRADEWELL.
O rare!

LUKE.   Then sitting at the table with
The braveries of the kingdom, you shall hear
Occurrents from all corners of the world,
The plots, the counsels, the designs of princes,
And freely censure 'em; the city wits   90
Cried up, or decried, as their passions lead 'em;
Judgment having nought to do there.

YOUNG TRADEWELL.   Admirable!

LUKE.

My lord no sooner shall rise out of his chair,
The gaming lord I mean, but you may boldly
By the privilege of a gamester fill his room,   95
For in play you are all fellows; have your knife
As soon in the pheasant; drink your health as freely,
And striking in a lucky hand or two,
Buy out your time.

YOUNG TRADEWELL.   This may be: but suppose
We should be known.

LUKE.   Have money and good clothes,   100
And you may pass invisible. Or if
You love a madam-punk, and your wide nostril
Be taken with the scent of cambric smocks,
Wrought and perfum'd—

YOUNG GOLDWIRE.   There, there, Master Luke,
There lies my road of happiness.

---

80. *lechery*] pleasure.
81. *ordinary*] cf. I.iii.7, note.
81. *cap-a-pe*] from head to foot.
87. *braveries*] gallants.
95. *fill . . . room*] take his place.
99. *time*] time remaining to complete the term of apprenticeship.
104. *Wrought*] embroidered.

LUKE.   Enjoy it,   105
    And pleasures stol'n being sweetest, apprehend
    The raptures of being hurried in a coach
    To Brainford, Staines, or Barnet.
YOUNG GOLDWIRE.   'Tis enchanting,
    I have prov'd it.
LUKE.   Hast thou?
YOUNG GOLDWIRE.   Yes, in all these places
    I have had my several pagans billeted   110
    For my own tooth, and after ten-pound suppers,
    The curtains drawn, my fiddlers playing all night
    "The Shaking of the Sheets," which I have danc'd
    Again and again with my cockatrice. Master Luke,
    You shall be of my counsel, and we two sworn brothers,   115
    And therefore I'll be open. I am out now
    Six hundred in the cash, yet if on a sudden
    I should be call'd to account, I have a trick
    How to evade it, and make up the sum.
YOUNG TRADEWELL.
    Is't possible?
LUKE.   You can instruct your tutor.   120
    How, how, good Tom?
YOUNG GOLDWIRE.   Why, look you. We cash-keepers
    Hold correspondence, supply one another
    On all occasions. I can borrow for a week
    Two hundred pounds of one, as much of a second,
    A third lays down the rest, and when they want,   125
    As my master's moneys come in, I do repay it:
    Ka me, ka thee.

120. instruct] *Mason;* intrust *Q.*

---

108. *Brainford*] the old spelling of Brentford, a town in Middlesex, eight
miles west of London.
    108. *Staines*] a town in Middlesex, seventeen miles west of London.
    108. *Barnet*] a town in Hertfordshire, eleven miles northwest of London.
    110. *pagans*] prostitutes.
    111. *For . . . tooth*] for my own pleasure.
    113. "*The Shaking of the Sheets*"] the name of a seventeenth-century dance.
The title was a common expression for sexual intercourse.
    114. *cockatrice*] whore.   115. *of my counsel*] in my confidence.
    127. *Ka me, ka thee*] "help me and I'll help thee."

LUKE.   An excellent knot! 'tis pity
It e'er should be unloos'd; for me it shall not.
You are shown the way, friend Tradewell, you may make
    use on't,
Or freeze in the warehouse, and keep company   130
With the cater Holdfast.

YOUNG TRADEWELL.   No, I am converted.
A Barbican broker will furnish me with outside,
And then a crash at the ordinary!

YOUNG GOLDWIRE.   I am for
The lady you saw this morning, who indeed is
My proper recreation.

LUKE.   Go to, Tom,   135
What did you make me?

YOUNG GOLDWIRE.   I'll do as much for you,
Employ me when you please.

LUKE.   If you are inquired for,
I will excuse you both.

YOUNG TRADEWELL.   Kind Master Luke!

YOUNG GOLDWIRE.

We'll break my master to make you. You know—

LUKE.

I cannot love money. Go, boys!

              [*Exeunt* Young Goldwire *and* Young Tradewell.]
                      When time serves   140
It shall appear, I have another end in't.   [*Exit.*]

[II.ii]
Enter Lord [Lacy], Sir John, [Sir Maurice] Lacy, Plenty, Lady
[Frugal], Anne, Mary, Milliscent.

SIR JOHN.

Ten thousand pounds apiece I'll make their portions,

141. *Exit.*] *Gifford; Exeunt Q.*   [II.ii]
                                 II.ii] *no scene division in Q.*

---

131. *cater*] caterer, purveyor.
132. *Barbican*] "a good broad Street, well inhabited by Tradesmen,
especially Salesmen for Apparel, both new and old" (Strype, Book III,
p. 93).
132. *outside*] external garments.

And after my decease it shall be double,
Provided you assure them for their jointures
Eight hundred pounds per annum, and entail
A thousand more upon the heirs male   5
Begotten on their bodies.

LORD LACY.   Sir, you bind us
To very strict conditions.

PLENTY.   You, my lord,
May do as you please: but to me it seems strange,
We should conclude of portions, and of jointures,
Before our hearts are settled.

LADY FRUGAL.   You say right.   10
There are counsels of more moment and importance
On the making up of marriages to be
Consider'd duly, than the portion or the jointures,
In which a mother's care must be exacted,
And I by special privilege may challenge   15
A casting voice.

LORD LACY.   How's this?

LADY FRUGAL.   Even so, my lord;
In these affairs I govern.

LORD LACY.   Give you way to't?

SIR JOHN.
I must, my lord.

LADY FRUGAL.   'Tis fit he should, and shall.
You may consult of something else, this province
Is wholly mine.

SIR MAURICE.   By the city custom, madam?   20

LADY FRUGAL.
Yes, my young sir, and both must look my daughters
Will hold it by my copy.

PLENTY.   Brave, i' faith!

SIR JOHN.
Give her leave to talk, we have the power to do;
And now touching the business we last talk'd of,

10.] *Q contains marginal S.D.* "*A
chair set out.*"

---

22. *copy*] copyhold (tenure of lands that were part of a manor was said
to be "by copy," i.e., according to the copy of the manorial court-roll).

In private if you please.

LORD LACY.   'Tis well remember'd;   25
You shall take your own way, madam.

Exeunt Lord [Lacy] *and* Sir John.

SIR MAURICE.   What strange lecture
Will she read unto us?

LADY FRUGAL.   Such as wisdom warrants
From the superior bodies. Is Stargaze ready
With his several schemes?

MILLISCENT.   Yes, madam, and attends
Your pleasure.   *Exit* Milliscent.

SIR MAURICE.   Stargaze, lady: what is he?   30

LADY FRUGAL.
Call him in. You shall first know him, then admire him
For a man of many parts, and those parts rare ones.
He's every thing, indeed; parcel physician,
And as such prescribes my diet, and foretells
My dreams when I eat potatoes; parcel poet,   35
And sings encomiums to my virtues sweetly;
My antecedent, or my gentleman usher,
And as the stars move, with that due proportion
He walks before me; but an absolute master
In the calculation of nativities,   40
Guided by that ne'er-erring science call'd
Judicial astrology.

PLENTY.   Stargaze! sure
I have a penny almanac about me
Inscrib'd to you, as to his patroness,
In his name publish'd.

LADY FRUGAL.   Keep it as a jewel.   45
Some statesmen that I will not name are wholly
Governed by his predictions, for they serve

---

29. *schemes*] diagrams showing the relative positions of the heavenly bodies at the time of a person's birth.

35. *potatoes*] the reference is to the yam or sweet potato. It was thought to have aphrodisiacal qualities.

37. *antecedent*] one who goes before.

42. *Judicial astrology*] "a Science pretending to judge of, and foretell future Events, by observing the Position and Influences of the Stars, etc." (Bailey).

For any latitude in Christendom,
As well as our own climate.

Enter Milliscent *and* Stargaze, *with two schemes.*

SIR MAURICE.   I believe so.
PLENTY.
Must we couple by the almanac?
LADY FRUGAL.   Be silent,   50
And e'er we do articulate, much more
Grow to a full conclusion, instruct us
Whether this day and hour, by the planets, promise
Happy success in marriage.
STARGAZE.   *In omni*
Parte, et toto.
PLENTY.   Good learn'd sir, in English;   55
And since it is resolved we must be coxcombs,
Make us so in our own language.
STARGAZE.   You are pleasant:
Thus in our vulgar tongue then.
LADY FRUGAL.   Pray you observe him.
STARGAZE.
Venus in the west angle, the house of marriage the seventh
house, in trine of Mars, in conjunction of Luna, and Mars   60
almuten, or lord of the horoscope.
PLENTY.
Hoy-day!
LADY FRUGAL.
The angels' language! I am ravish'd! Forward.
STARGAZE.
Mars, as I said, lord of the horoscope, or geniture, in mutual

---

49. S.P. SIR MAURICE.] *Dodsley;*   57. our] *Q (corrected); not in Q*
speech assigned to Lady Frugal Q.   *(uncorrected).*

---

51. *articulate*] "enter into articles of agreement" (Nares).
54–55. *In . . . toto*] "in all parts and the whole."
60. *trine*] "the aspect of two heavenly bodies which are a third part of
the zodiac, i.e., 120°, distant from each other" (*OED*).
61. *almuten*] "The ruling planet in the horoscope" (*OED*).
62. *Hoy-day*] an exclamation of surprise.
64. *geniture*] nativity.

reception of each other, she in her exaltation, and he in his   65
triplicity trine, and face, assure a fortunate combination to
Hymen, excellent prosperous and happy.

LADY FRUGAL.

Kneel, and give thanks.   *The women kneel.*

SIR MAURICE.   For what we understand not?

PLENTY.

And have as little faith in't?

LADY FRUGAL.   Be credulous;

To me, 'tis oracle.   70

STARGAZE.

Now for the sovereignty of my future ladies, your daughters,
after they are married.

PLENTY.

Wearing the breeches, you mean?

LADY FRUGAL.   Touch that point home,

It is a principal one, and with London ladies
Of main consideration.   75

STARGAZE.

This is infallible: Saturn out of all dignities in his detriment
and fall, combust: and Venus in the south angle elevated
above him, lady of both their nativities, in her essential and
accidental dignities; occidental from the sun, oriental from
the angle of the east, in cazimi of the sun, in her joy, and   80

---

65. *reception*] "The fact of each of two planets being received into the
other's house, exaltation, or other dignity" (*OED*).

65. *exaltation*] "The place of a planet in the zodiac in which it was
supposed to exert its greatest influence" (*OED*).

66. *triplicity*] "the Division of the Signs [of the zodiac] according to the
Number of the [four] Elements [earth, water, air, fire], each Division
consisting of three Signs" (Bailey).

66. *face*] the third part (ten degrees) of a sign of the zodiac.

76. *dignities*] "Dignity" is "a situation of a planet in which its influence
is heightened" (*OED*).

76. *detriment*] "The position or condition of a planet when in the sign
opposite its house; a condition of weakness" (*OED*).

77. *combust*] "The being within 8° 30′ of the [sun], which is said to burn
up those planets near him, so that they lose their power" (Lilly, p. 339).

80. *in cazimi*] "An old astrological term, denoting the centre or middle
of the sun. A planet is said to be in *cazimi* when not distant from the sun,
either in longitude or latitude, above 17 minutes; or the apparent semi-
diameter of the sun, and of the planet" (Nares).

free from the malevolent beams of infortunes; in a sign
commanding, and Mars in a constellation obeying; she
fortunate, and he dejected: the disposers of marriage in
the radix of the native in feminine figures, argue, foretell,
and declare rule, preeminence, and absolute sovereignty in   85
women.

SIR MAURICE.

Is't possible!

STARGAZE.

'Tis drawn, I assure you, from the aphorisms of the old Chaldeans, Zoroastes the first and greatest magician, Mercurius
Trismegistus, the later Ptolemy, and the everlasting prog-   90
nosticator, old Erra Pater.

LADY FRUGAL.

Are you yet satisfied?

PLENTY.   In what?

LADY FRUGAL.   That you
Are bound to obey your wives, it being so
Determin'd by the stars, against whose influence
There is no opposition.

PLENTY.   Since I must   95
Be married by the almanac, as I may be,
'Twere requisite the services and duties
Which, as you say, I must pay to my wife,
Were set down in the calendar.

SIR MAURICE.   With the date
Of my apprenticeship.

85. declare rule, preeminence, and]   preheminence and Q.
Gifford; declare preheminence, rule,

88–89. *Chaldeans*] ancient astrologers.

89. *Zoroastes*] "*Justin* says positively, that *Zoroaster* was King of the
Bactrians, and the Inventor of *Magick*" (Bailey).

89–90. *Mercurius Trismegistus*] a Latinized version of the name of Hermes
Trismegistus ("thrice greatest Hermes"), by which Thoth, the Egyptian
god of wisdom was called.

90. *Ptolemy*] Claudius Ptolemaeus, Alexandrian astronomer (active A.D.
121–151).

91. *Erra Pater*] "This was formerly very current as the name of an old
astrologer, but who was meant by it cannot so easily be determined" (Nares).

LADY FRUGAL.   Make your demands;   100
   I'll sit as moderatrix, if they press you
   With over-hard conditions.
SIR MAURICE.   Mine hath the van;
   I stand your charge, sweet.
STARGAZE.   Silence.
ANNE.   I require first
   (And that since 'tis in fashion with kind husbands,
   In civil manners you must grant) my will   105
   In all things whatsoever, and that will
   To be obey'd, not argu'd.
LADY FRUGAL.   And good reason.
PLENTY.
   A gentle *imprimis*!
SIR MAURICE.   This in gross contains all;
   But your special items, lady.
ANNE.   When I am one
   (And you are honor'd to be styl'd my husband)   110
   To urge my having my page, my gentleman usher,
   My woman sworn to my secrets, my caroch
   Drawn by six Flanders mares, my coachmen, grooms,
   Postillion, and footmen.
SIR MAURICE.   Is there ought else
   To be demanded?
ANNE.   Yes, sir, mine own doctor;   115
   French and Italian cooks; musicians, songsters,
   And a chaplain that must preach to please my fancy;
   A friend at court to place me at a masque;
   The private box took up at a new play
   For me, and my retinue; a fresh habit,   120
   Of a fashion never seen before, to draw
   The gallants' eyes that sit on the stage upon me;
   Some decay'd lady for my parasite,
   To flatter me, and rail at other madams;
   And there ends my ambition.

---

102. *van*] vanguard.
108. *imprimis*] "in the first place" (with reference to Anne's "first"
requirement, l. 103).
112. *caroch*] a large coach.

SIR MAURICE.   Your desires   125
    Are modest, I confess.
ANNE.   These toys subscrib'd to,
    And you continuing an obedient husband
    Upon all fit occasions, you shall find me
    A most indulgent wife.
LADY FRUGAL.   You have said; give place
    And hear your younger sister.
PLENTY.   If she speak   130
    Her language, may the great fiend, booted and spurr'd,
    With a scythe at his girdle, as the Scotchman says,
    Ride headlong down her throat.
SIR MAURICE.   Curse not the judge
    Before you hear the sentence.
MARY.   In some part
    My sister hath spoke well for the city pleasures,   135
    But I am for the country's, and must say,
    Under correction, in her demands she was
    Too modest.
SIR MAURICE.   How like you this exordium?
PLENTY.
    Too modest, with a mischief!
MARY.   Yes, too modest:
    I know my value, and prize it to the worth,   140
    My youth, my beauty—
PLENTY.   How your glass deceives you!
MARY.
    —The greatness of the portion I bring with me,
    And the sea of happiness that from me flows to you.
SIR MAURICE.
    She bears up close.
MARY.   And can you in your wisdom,
    Or rustical simplicity, imagine   145
    You have met some innocent country girl, that never
    Look'd further than her father's farm, nor knew more
    Than the price of corn in the market; or at what rate

    131–133. *may ... throat*] "The Devil run through you booted and
spurred with a scythe on his back" (Tilley, D 264).
    144. *She ... close*] she upholds (her point of view) firmly.

Beef went a stone? that would survey your dairy,
And bring in mutton out of cheese and butter?   150
That could give directions at what time of the moon
To cut her cocks, for capons against Christmas,
Or when to raise up goslings?

PLENTY.   These are arts
Would not misbecome you, though you should put in
Obedience and duty.

MARY.   Yes, and patience,   155
To sit like a fool at home, and eye your thrashers;
Then make provision for your slavering hounds,
When you come drunk from an alehouse after hunting,
With your clowns and comrades as if all were yours,
You the lord paramount, and I the drudge;   160
The case, sir, must be otherwise.

PLENTY.   How, I beseech you?

MARY.

Marry, thus: I will not like my sister challenge
What's useful or superfluous from my husband,
That's base all o'er. Mine shall receive from me,
What I think fit. I'll have the state convey'd   165
Into my hands, and he put to his pension,
Which the wise viragos of our climate practice;
I will receive your rents—

PLENTY.   You shall be hang'd first.

MARY.

—Make sale, or purchase. Nay, I'll have my neighbors
Instructed, when a passenger shall ask,   170
"Whose house is this?" though you stand by, to answer,
"The Lady Plenty's." Or, "Who owes this manor?"
"The Lady Plenty." "Whose sheep are these? Whose
     oxen?"
"The Lady Plenty's."

PLENTY.   A plentiful pox upon you!

---

149. *stone*] "A measure of weight, usually equal to 14 pounds avoirdupois"
(*OED*).
152. *against*] in preparation for.
167. *viragos*] female warriors.
172. *owes*] owns.

MARY.
    And when I have children, if it be inquir'd   175
    By a stranger whose they are, they shall still echo,
    "My Lady Plenty's," the husband never thought on.
PLENTY.
    In their begetting, I think so.
MARY.   Since you'll marry
    In the city for our wealth, in justice we
    Must have the country's sovereignty.
PLENTY.   And we nothing.   180
MARY.
    A nag of forty shillings, a couple of spaniels,
    With a sparhawk, is sufficient, and these too,
    As you shall behave yourself, during my pleasure,
    I will not greatly stand on. I have said, sir,
    Now if you like me, so.
LADY FRUGAL.   At my entreaty,   185
    The articles shall be easier.
PLENTY.   Shall they, i' faith?
    Like bitch, like whelps.
SIR MAURICE.   Use fair words.
PLENTY.   I cannot;
    I have read of a house of pride, and now I have found one;
    A whirlwind overturn it!
SIR MAURICE.   On these terms,
    Will your minxship be a lady?
PLENTY.   A lady in a morris;.   190
    I'll wed a pedlar's punk first—
SIR MAURICE.   Tinker's trull,
    A beggar without a smock.
PLENTY.   Let Monsieur Almanac,
    Since he is so cunning with his Jacob's staff,
    Find you out a husband in a bowling alley.

---

182. *sparhawk*] sparrowhawk.
184. *I . . . on*] I will not raise difficulties (as to Plenty's possessing the nag, spaniels, and sparhawk).
190. *morris*] morris-dance.
191. *trull*] trollop.
193. *Jacob's staff*] an instrument used for taking the altitude of the sun.

SIR MAURICE.
  The general pimp to a brothel.
PLENTY.   Though that now   195
  All the loose desires of man were rak'd up in me,
  And no means but thy maidenhead left to quench 'em,
  I would turn cinders, or the next sow-gelder,
  On my life, should lib me, rather than embrace thee.
ANNE.
  Wooing do you call this?
MARY.   A bear-baiting rather.   200
PLENTY.
  Were you worried, you deserve it, and I hope
  I shall live to see it.
SIR MAURICE.   I'll not rail, nor curse you,
  Only this: you are pretty peats, and your great portions
  Adds much unto your handsomeness, but as
  You would command your husbands you are beggars,   205
  Deform'd and ugly.
LADY FRUGAL.   Hear me.
PLENTY.   Not a word more.
                  Exeunt [Sir Maurice] Lacy *and* Plenty.
ANNE.
  I ever thought 'twoud come to this.
MARY.   We may
  Lead apes in hell for husbands, if you bind us
  T' articulate thus with our suitors.   *Both speak weeping.*
STARGAZE.   Now the cloud breaks,
  And the storm will fall on me.
LADY FRUGAL.   You rascal! juggler!   210
                  She breaks his head, and beats him.

---

  199. *lib*] castrate.
  201. *worried*] irritated, provoked, as a bear (line 200) would be in the
baiting.
  203. *peat*] "A delicate person; usually applied to a young female, but
often ironically, as meaning a spoiled, pampered favourite" (Nares).
  208. *Lead apes in hell*] the proverbial employment of old maids in the
next world. "As *ape* occasionally meant a fool, it probably meant that
those coquettes who made fools of men, and led them about without real
intention of marriage, would have them still to lead against their will
hereafter" (Nares).

STARGAZE.
   Dear madam.
LADY FRUGAL.   Hold you intelligence with the stars,
   And thus deceive me!
STARGAZE.   My art cannot err;
   If it does, I'll burn my astrolabe. In mine own star
   I did foresee this broken head, and beating;
   And now your ladyship sees, as I do feel it,   215
   It could not be avoided.
LADY FRUGAL.   Did you?
STARGAZE.   Madam,
   Have patience but a week, and if you find not
   All my predictions true touching your daughters,
   And a change of fortune to yourself, a rare one,
   Turn me out of doors. These are not the men the planets   220
   Appointed for their husbands; there will come
   Gallants of another metal.
MILLISCENT.   Once more trust him.
ANNE. MARY.
   Do, lady mother.
LADY FRUGAL.   I am vex'd, look to it;
   Turn o'er your books; if once again you fool me,
   You shall graze elsewhere: come girls.
                     Exeunt [Lady Frugal, Anne, Mary, Milliscent.]
STARGAZE.   I am glad I scap'd thus.   [*Exit.*] 225

[II.iii]   *Enter* Lord [Lacy] *and* Sir John [Frugal].

LORD LACY.
   The plot shows very likely.
SIR JOHN.   I repose
   My principal trust in your lordship; 'twill prepare
   The physic I intend to minister
   To my wife and daughters.
LORD LACY.   I will do my parts
   To set it off to the life.

_____

   213. *astrolabe*] "a Mathematical Instrument, to take the Altitude of the
Sun or Stars" (Bailey).

Enter [Sir Maurice] Lacy *and* Plenty.

SIR JOHN.   It may produce   5
  A scene of no vulgar mirth. Here come the suitors;
  When we understand how they relish my wife's humors,
  The rest is feasible.
LORD LACY.   Their looks are cloudy.
SIR JOHN.
  How sits the wind? Are you ready to launch forth
  Into this sea of marriage?
PLENTY.   Call it rather   10
  A whirlpool of afflictions.
SIR MAURICE.   If you please
  To enjoin me to it, I will undertake
  To find the north passage to the Indies sooner
  Than plow with your proud heifer.
PLENTY.   I will make
  A voyage to hell first.—
SIR JOHN.   How, sir!
PLENTY.   —And court Proserpine   15
  In the sight of Pluto, his three-headed porter
  Cerberus standing by, and all the furies
  With their whips to scourge me for't, than say, "I Jeffrey
  Take you Mary for my wife."
LORD LACY.   Why what's the matter?
SIR MAURICE.
  The matter is, the mother (with your pardon,   20
  I cannot but speak so much) is a most insufferable,
  Proud, insolent lady.
PLENTY.   And the daughters worse.
  The dam in·years had th' advantage to be wicked,
  But they were so in her belly.
SIR MAURICE.   I must tell you,
  With reverence to your wealth, I do begin   25
  To think you of the same leaven.
PLENTY.   Take my counsel;
  'Tis safer for your credit to profess

19. you] *Coxeter;* your *Q.*

---

26. *of the same leaven*] of the same sort of character.

Yourself a cuckold, and upon record,
Than say they are your daughters.

SIR JOHN.   You go too far, sir.

SIR MAURICE.
They have so articl'd with us—

PLENTY.   And will not take us   30
For their husbands, but their slaves, and so aforehand
They do profess they'll use us.

SIR JOHN.   Leave this heat:
Though they are mine, I must tell you, the perverseness
Of their manners (which they did not take from me,
But from their mother) qualified, they deserve   35
Your equals.

SIR MAURICE.   True, but what's bred in the bone
Admits no hope of cure.

PLENTY.   Though saints and angels
Were their physicians.

SIR JOHN.   You conclude too fast.

PLENTY.
God be wi' you! I'll travel three years, but I'll bury
This shame that lives upon me.

SIR MAURICE.   With your license,   40
I'll keep him company.

LORD LACY.   Who shall furnish you
For your expenses?

PLENTY.   He shall not need your help,
My purse is his; we were rivals, but now friends,
And will live and die so.

SIR MAURICE.   Ere we go, I'll pay
My duty as a son.

PLENTY.   And till then leave you.   45

Exeunt [Sir Maurice] Lacy *and* Plenty.

LORD LACY.
They are strangely mov'd.

SIR JOHN.   What's wealth, accompanied
With disobedience in a wife and children?
My heart will break.

39. be wi'] *Gifford;* bowy *Q*.

_____

40. *license*] permission.

-43-

LORD LACY.   Be comforted, and hope better;
    We'll ride abroad; the fresh air and discourse
    May yield us new inventions.

SIR JOHN.   You are noble,   50
    And shall in all things, as you please, command me.   *Exeunt.*

[III.i]   *Enter* Shave'em *and* Secret.

SECRET.
    Dead doings, daughter.

SHAVE'EM.   Doings! sufferings, mother:
    Men have forgot what doing is;
    And such as have to pay for what they do,
    Are impotent, or eunuchs.

SECRET.   You have a friend yet,
    And a striker too, I take it.

SHAVE'EM.   Goldwire is so, and comes   5
    To me by stealth, and as he can steal, maintains me
    In clothes, I grant; but alas, dame, what's one friend?
    I would have a hundred for every hour, and use,
    And change of humor I am in, a fresh one.
    'Tis a flock of sheep that makes a lean wolf fat,   10
    And not a single lambkin. I am starv'd,
    Starv'd in my pleasures. I know not what a coach is,
    To hurry me to the Burse, or Old Exchange.
    The neathouse for muskmelons, and the gardens
    Where we traffic for asparagus, are to me   15
    In the other world.

4–5.] *Q contains marginal S.D.*
"Musick come/ down."

---

2. *doing*] For the sexual implication of the word, see Eric Partridge,
Shakespeare's Bawdy (New York, 1960), p. 103.
   5. *striker*] fornicator.
  13. *the Burse*] Britain's Burse, or the New Exchange.
  14. *neathouse*] literally, "cow-house," applied specially to the site of
some cowsheds on the bank of the Thames west of Vauxhall Bridge. "The
Neat Houses are a Parcel of Houses, most seated on the banks of the River
Thames, and inhabited by Gardiners; for which it is of Note, for the supplying
London and *Westminster* Markets with *Asparagus, Artichoaks, Cauliflowers,
Musemelons*, and the like useful Things that the Earth produceth . . ."
(Strype, Book VI, p. 67).

SECRET.   There are other places, lady,
Where you might find customers.
SHAVE'EM.   You would have me foot it
To the dancing of the ropes, sit a whole afternoon there
In expectation of nuts and pippins;
Gape round about me, and yet not find a chapman   20
That in courtesy will bid a chop of mutton,
Or a pint of drum-wine for me.
SECRET.   You are so impatient!
But I can tell you news will comfort you,
And the whole sisterhood.
SHAVE'EM.   What's that?
SECRET.   I am told
Two ambassadors are come over: a French monsieur,   25
And a Venetian, one of the clarissimi,
A hot-rein'd marmoset. Their followers,
For their countries' honor, after a long vacation,
Will make a full term with us.
SHAVE'EM.   They indeed are
Our certain and best customers: *Knock within.*
                              Who knocks there?   30
(*Within*) RAMBLE.
Open the door.
SECRET.   What are you?
(*Within*) RAMBLE.   Ramble.
(*Within*) SCUFFLE.   Scuffle.
(*Within*) RAMBLE.
Your constant visitants.

17–19. *You would . . . pippins*] Shave'em interprets Secret to suggest that
she should look for customers at a theater, notorious haunt of prostitutes,
where rope dancers often performed. There is a quibble on the word "foot";
used as a verb, it is often, in Elizabethan usage, a euphemism for "copulate"
(see Partridge, p. 115). Elizabethan audiences were celebrated for munch-
ing on nuts and apples ("pippins"), sold in the theater, during a performance.
21. *mutton*] a cant term for prostitute.
22. *drum-wine*] "wine sold 'by the drum'," i.e., "by public announcement" (*OED*, conj.).
26. *clarissimi*] grandees of Venice.
27. *A hot-rein'd marmoset*] "i.e., a monkey, a libidinous animal" (Gifford).

SHAVE'EM.   Let 'em not in.
I know 'em swaggering, suburban roarers,
Sixpenny truckers.
(*Within*) RAMBLE.   Down go all your windows,
And your neighbors too shall suffer.
(*Within*) SCUFFLE.   Force the doors.   35
SECRET.   They are outlaws, Mistress Shave'em, and there is
No remedy against 'em. What should you fear?
They are but men; lying at your close ward,
You have foil'd their betters.
SHAVE'EM.   Out, you bawd! You care not
Upon what desperate service you employ me,   40
Nor with whom, so you have your fee.
SECRET.   Sweet ladybird,
Sing a milder key.

                    Enter Ramble *and* Scuffle.

SCUFFLE.   Are you grown proud?
RAMBLE.
I knew you a waistcoateer in the garden alleys,
And would come to a sailor's whistle.
SECRET.   Good sir Ramble,
Use her not roughly. She is very tender.   45
RAMBLE.
Rank and rotten, is she not?   [Shave'em] *draws her knife.*
SHAVE'EM.   Your spittle rogueships
                    Ramble [*draws*] *his sword.*
Shall not make me so.
SECRET.   As you are a man, squire Scuffle,
Step in between 'em. A weapon of that length
Was ne'er drawn in my house.
SHAVE'EM.   Let him come on,

46. S.D. Shave'em] *She Q.*

_____

33. *suburbian*] suburban, "with reference to the licentious life of the
[seventeenth-century London] suburbs" (*OED*).
33. *roarers*] riotous bullies.
34. *truckers*] hagglers.
43. *waistcoateer*] whore.
46. *spittle*] a hospital for the diseased, generally for those suffering from
venereal disease.

I'll scour it in your guts, you dog.

RAMBLE.   You brach,   50
Are you turn'd mankind? You forgot I gave you,
When we last join'd issue, twenty pound.

SHAVE'EM.
O'er night, and kick'd it out of me in the morning.
I was then a novice, but I know to make
My game now. Fetch the constable.

Enter [Young] Goldwire *like a Justice of Peace,* Ding'em *like a Constable,*
the Musicians like Watchmen.

SECRET.   Ah me!   55
Here's one unsent for, and a justice of peace too.

SHAVE'EM.
I'll hang you both, you rascals—I can but ride—
You for the purse you cut in Paul's at a sermon.
I have smok'd you! And you for the bacon you took on the
          highway
From the poor market woman as she rode from Rumford.   60

RAMBLE.
Mistress Shave'em.

SCUFFLE.   Mistress Secret, on our knees
We beg your pardon.

RAMBLE.   Set a ransom on us.

SECRET.
We cannot stand trifling. If you mean to save them,
Shut them out at the back door.

SHAVE'EM.   First, for punishment,
They shall leave their cloaks behind 'em, and in sign   65
I am their sovereign, and they my vassals,
For homage kiss my shoe-sole, rogues, and vanish.
                              Exeunt Ramble *and* Scuffle.

62. S.P. RAMBLE.] *Coxeter; speech*
assigned to Scuffle Q.

---

51. *mankind*] mannish, impudent, ferocious.
57. *I can but ride*] i.e., be carted for a strumpet.
59. *smok'd*] exposed.
60. *Rumford*] a town in Essex, twelve miles northeast of London.

YOUNG GOLDWIRE.
  My brave virago! The coast's clear. Strike up.
            [Young] Goldwire, *and the rest discovered.*
SHAVE'EM.
  My Goldwire made a justice!
SECRET.   And your scout
  Turn'd constable, and the musicians watchmen!   70
YOUNG GOLDWIRE.
  We come not to fright you, but to make you merry.
  A light lavolta!   *They dance.*
SHAVE'EM.   I am tir'd. No more.
  This was your device.
DING'EM.   Wholly his own. He is
  No pig-sconce, mistress.
SECRET.   He has an excellent headpiece.
YOUNG GOLDWIRE.
  Fie no, not I! Your jeering gallants say   75
  We citizens have no wit.
DING'EM.   He dies that says so.
  This was a masterpiece.
YOUNG GOLDWIRE.   A trifling stratagem,
  Not worth the talking of.
SHAVE'EM.   I must kiss thee for it
  Again, and again.
DING'EM.   Make much of her. Did you know
  What suitors she had since she saw you—
YOUNG GOLDWIRE.   I' the way of marriage? 80
DING'EM.
  Yes, sir; for marriage, and the other thing too;
  The commodity is the same. An Irish lord offer'd her
  Five pound a week.
SECRET.   And a cashier'd captain, half
  Of his entertainment.
DING'EM.   And a new-made courtier,
  The next suit he could beg.

---

72. *lavolta*] "A kind of dance for two persons, consisting a good deal in high and active bounds" (Nares).
74. *pig-sconce*] pig-headed fellow.
84. *entertainment*] wages.

YOUNG GOLDWIRE.   And did my sweet one   85
    Refuse all this for me?
SHAVE'EM.   Weep not for joy,
    'Tis true. Let others talk of lords, and commanders,
    And country heirs for their servants; but give me
    My gallant prentice. He parts with his money
    So civilly, and demurely; keeps no account   90
    Of his expenses, and comes ever furnish'd.
    I know thou hast brought money to make up
    My gown and petticoat, with th' appurtenances.
YOUNG GOLDWIRE.
    I have it here, duck; thou shalt want for nothing.
SHAVE'EM.
    Let the chamber be perfum'd—[to Ding'em] and get you,
    sirrah,   95
    His cap and pantables ready.
YOUNG GOLDWIRE.   There's for thee,
    And thee: that for a banquet.
SECRET.   And a caudle
    Against you rise.
YOUNG GOLDWIRE.   There.
SHAVE'EM.   Usher us up in state.
YOUNG GOLDWIRE.
    You will be constant.
SHAVE'EM.   Thou art the whole world to me.
              Exeunt, wanton music played before 'em.

[III.ii]   *Enter* Luke.
(*Within*) ANNE.
    Where is this uncle?
(*Within*) LADY FRUGAL.   Call this beadsman-brother:
    He hath forgot attendance.
(*Within*) MARY.   Seek him out:
    Idleness spoils him.

---

96. *pantables*] "A sort of high shoe, or slipper" (Nares).
    97. *caudle*] "a Confection made of Ale, or Wine, Sugar, and Spices, to be drank hot" (Bailey).
    98. *Against*] before.
[III.ii]
    1. *beadsman*] almsman.

LUKE.　　　　　　　　I deserve much more
Than their scorn can load me with, and 'tis but justice
That I should live the family's drudge, design'd　　　　　　5
To all the sordid offices their pride
Imposes on me; since if now I sat
A judge in mine own cause, I should conclude
I am not worth their pity. Such as want
Discourse, and judgment, and through weakness fall,　　　10
May merit man's compassion; but I,
That knew profuseness of expense the parent
Of wretched poverty, her fatal daughter,
To riot out mine own, to live upon
The alms of others, steering on a rock　　　　　　　　15
I might have shunn'd! O heaven! 'tis not fit
I should look upward, much less hope for mercy.

Enter Lady [Frugal], Anne, Mary, Stargaze, *and* Milliscent.

LADY FRUGAL.
What are you devising, sir?
ANNE.　　　　　　　　　My uncle is much given
To his devotion.
MARY.　　　　　　　And takes time to mumble
A paternoster to himself.
LADY FRUGAL.　　　　　　Know you where　　　　　　20
Your brother is? It better would become you
(Your means of life depending wholly on him)
To give your attendance.
LUKE.　　　　　　　　In my will I do:
But since he rode forth yesterday with Lord Lacy,
I have not seen him.
LADY FRUGAL.　　　　And why went not you　　　　　25
By his stirrup? How do you look! Were his eyes clos'd,
You'd be glad of such employment.
LUKE.　　　　　　　　　　'Twas his pleasure
I should wait your commands, and those I am ever
Most ready to receive.
LADY FRUGAL.　　　　I know you can speak well,
But say and do.

---

10. *Discourse*] faculty of reasoning.

Enter Lord Lacy *with a will.*

LUKE.   Here comes my lord.

LADY FRUGAL.   Further off: 30
You are no companion for him, and his business
Aims not at you, as I take it.

LUKE *(aside)*.   Can I live
In this base condition!

LADY FRUGAL.   I hop'd, my lord,
You had brought Master Frugal with you, for I must ask
An account of him from you.

LORD LACY.   I can give it, lady;   35
But with the best discretion of a woman,
And a strong fortified patience, I desire you
To give it hearing.

LUKE.   My heart beats.

LADY FRUGAL.
My lord, you much amaze me.

LORD LACY.
I shall astonish you. The noble merchant,   40
Who living was for his integrity
And upright dealing (a rare miracle
In a rich citizen) London's best honor;
Is—I am loath to speak it.

LUKE.   Wondrous strange!

LADY FRUGAL.
I do suppose the worst, not dead I hope?   45

LORD LACY.
Your supposition's true, your hopes are false.
He's dead.

LADY FRUGAL.   Ay me!

ANNE.   My father!

MARY.   My kind father!

LUKE.
Now they insult not.

LORD LACY.   Pray hear me out.
He's dead. Dead to the world, and you. And now
Lives only to himself.

LUKE.   What riddle's this?   50

—51—

LADY FRUGAL.

    Act not the torturer in my afflictions;
    But make me understand the sum of all
    That I must undergo.

LORD LACY.   In few words take it:
    He is retir'd into a monastery
    Where he resolves to end his days.

LUKE.   More strange.   55

LORD LACY.

    I saw him take post for Dover, and the wind
    Sitting so fair, by this he's safe at Calice,
    And ere long will be at Louvain.

LADY FRUGAL.   Could I guess
    What were the motives that induc'd him to it,
    'Twere some allay to my sorrows.

LORD LACY.   I'll instruct you,   60
    And chide you into that knowledge. 'Twas your pride
    Above your rank, and stubborn disobedience
    Of these your daughters, in their milk suck'd from you:
    At home the harshness of his entertainment,
    You willfully forgetting that your all   65
    Was borrowed from him; and to hear abroad
    The imputations dispers'd upon you,
    And justly too, I fear, that drew him to
    This strict retirement: and thus much said for him,
    I am myself to accuse you.

LADY FRUGAL.   I confess   70
    A guilty cause to him, but in a thought,
    My lord, I ne'er wrong'd you.

LORD LACY.   In fact you have;
    The insolent disgrace you put upon
    My only son, and Master Plenty; men, that lov'd
    Your daughters in a noble way, to wash off   75
    The scandal, put a resolution in 'em
    For three years travel.

LADY FRUGAL.   I am much griev'd for it.

---

57. *Calice*] Calais.

LORD LACY.

    One thing I had forgot; your rigor to
His decayed brother, in which your flatteries,
Or sorceries, made him a co-agent with you,   80
Wrought not the least impression.

LUKE.   Humph! this sounds well.

LADY FRUGAL.

    'Tis now past help: after these storms, my lord,
A little calm, if you please.

LORD LACY.   If what I have told you
Show'd like a storm, what now I must deliver
Will prove a raging tempest. His whole estate   85
In lands and leases, debts and present moneys,
With all the movables he stood possess'd of,
With the best advice which he could get for gold
From his learned counsel, by this formal will
Is pass'd o'er to his brother. With it take   90
The key of his countinghouse. Not a groat left you,
Which you can call your own.

LADY FRUGAL.   Undone forever!

ANNE. MARY.

    What will become of us?

LUKE.   Humph!

    [Lady Frugal, Anne, *and* Mary *kneel to* Lord Lacy.]

LORD LACY.   The scene's chang'd,
And he that was your slave, by fate appointed
Your governor. You kneel to me in vain,   95
I cannot help you, I discharge the trust
Impos'd upon me. This humility
From him may gain remission, and perhaps
Forgetfulness of your barbarous usage to him.

LADY FRUGAL.

    Am I come to this?

LORD LACY.   Enjoy your own, good sir,   100
But use it with due reverence. I once heard you
Speak most divinely in the opposition
Of a revengeful humor; to these show it,
And such who then depended on the mercy
Of your brother, wholly now at your devotion,   105
And make good the opinion I held of you,

-53-

Of which I am most confident.

LUKE [*to* Lady Frugal, Anne, Mary].   Pray you rise,
 And rise with this assurance, I am still,
 As I was of late, your creature; and if rais'd
 In any thing, 'tis in my power to serve you,   110
 My will is still the same. —[*To* Lord Lacy.] O my lord!
 This heap of wealth which you possess me of,
 Which to a worldly man had been a blessing,
 And to the messenger might with justice challenge
 A kind of adoration, is to me   115
 A curse I cannot thank you for; and much less
 Rejoice in that tranquility of mind
 My brother's vows must purchase. I have made
 A dear exchange with him. He now enjoys
 My peace and poverty, the trouble of   120
 His wealth conferr'd on me, and that a burden
 Too heavy for my weak shoulders.
LORD LACY.   Honest soul,
 With what feeling he receives it.
LADY FRUGAL.   You shall have
 My best assistance, if you please to use it,
 To help you to support it.
LUKE.   By no means!   125
 The weight shall rather sink me, than you part
 With one short minute from those lawful pleasures
 Which you were born to, in your care to aid me.
 You shall have all abundance. In my nature
 I was ever liberal—my lord you know it—   130
 Kind, affable. And now methinks I see
 Before my face the jubilee of joy,
 When it is assur'd my brother lives in me,
 His debtors in full cups crown'd to my health,
 With paeans to my praise will celebrate.   135
 For they well know 'tis far from me to take
 The forfeiture of a bond. Nay, I shall blush,
 The interest never paid after three years,
 When I demand my principal. And his servants,
 Who from a slavish fear paid their obedience   140

140. their] *Mason;* her *Q.*

By him exacted, now when they are mine
Will grow familiar friends, and as such use me,
Being certain of the mildness of my temper,
Which my change of fortune, frequent in most men,
Hath not the power to alter.

LORD LACY.   Yet take heed, sir,   145
    You ruin it not with too much lenity,
    What his fit severity rais'd.

LADY FRUGAL.   And we fall from
    That height we have maintain'd.

LUKE.   I'll build it higher,
    To admiration higher. With disdain
    I look upon these habits, no way suiting   150
    The wife and daughters of a knighted citizen
    Bless'd with abundance.

LORD LACY.   There, sir, I join with you;
    A fit decorum must be kept, the court
    Distinguished from the city.

LUKE.   With your favor,
    I know what you would say, but give me leave   155
    In this to be your advocate. You are wide,
    Wide the whole region in what I purpose.
    Since all the titles, honors, long descents
    Borrow their gloss from wealth, the rich with reason
    May challenge their prerogatives. And it shall be   160
    My glory, nay a triumph to revive
    In the pomp that these shall shine, the memory
    Of the Roman matrons, who kept captive queens
    To be their handmaids. And when you appear
    Like Juno in full majesty, and my nieces   165
    Like Iris, Hebe, or what deities else
    Old poets fancy (your cramm'd wardrobes richer
    Than various nature's), and draw down the envy
    Of our western world upon you, only hold me

152. Bless'd] Q (corrected); Blessed Q
(uncorrected).
157. Wide the whole] Q (corrected);
The whole Q (uncorrected).

159. wealth, the] Q (corrected);
wealth ye'r Q (uncorrected).
167. cramm'd] Q (corrected); exam-
in'd Q (uncorrected).

156. wide] mistaken.

Your viligant Hermes with aerial wings,   170
My caduceus my strong zeal to serve you,
Press'd to fetch in all rarities may delight you,
And I am made immortal.

LORD LACY.   A strange frenzy!

LUKE.
Off with these rags, and then to bed. There dream
Of future greatness, which when you awake   175
I'll make a certain truth: but I must be
A doer, not a promiser. The performance
Requiring haste, I kiss your hands, and leave you.   *Exit* Luke.

LORD LACY.
Are we all turn'd statues? have his strange words charm'd us?
What muse you on, lady?

LADY FRUGAL.   Do not trouble me.   180

LORD LACY.
Sleep you too, young ones?

ANNE.   Swift-wing'd time till now
Was never tedious to me. Would 'twere night.

MARY.
Nay, morning rather.

LORD LACY.   Can you ground your faith
On such impossibilities? Have you so soon
Forgot your good husband?

LADY FRUGAL.   He was a vanity   185
I must no more remember.

LORD LACY.   Excellent!
You, your kind father?

ANNE.   Such an uncle never
Was read of in story!

LORD LACY.   Not one word in answer
Of my demands?

MARY.   You are but a lord; and know,
My thoughts soar higher.

LORD LACY.   Admirable! I will leave you   190
To your castles in the air.—[*Aside*]. When I relate this,
It will exceed belief, but he must know it.   *Exit* Lord [Lacy].

173. I] *Dodsley; not in Q.*   181. too] *Q (corrected); to Q (uncorrected).*

STARGAZE.
    Now I may boldly speak. May it please you, madam,
    To look upon your vassal; I foresaw this,
    The stars assur'd it.
LADY FRUGAL.   I begin to feel   195
    Myself another woman.
STARGAZE.   Now you shall find
    All my predictions true, and nobler matches
    Prepar'd for my young ladies.
MILLISCENT.   Princely husbands.
ANNE.
    I'll go no less.
MARY.   Not a word more;
    Provide my night-rail.
MILLISCENT.   What shall we be tomorrow!   *Exeunt* 200

[III.iii]   *Enter* Luke *with a key.*

LUKE.
    'Twas no fantastic object, but a truth,
    A real truth. Nor dream: I did not slumber,
    And could wake ever with a brooding eye
    To gaze upon't! It did endure the touch;
    I saw, and felt it. Yet what I beheld   5
    And handl'd oft, did so transcend belief
    (My wonder and astonishment pass'd o'er)
    I faintly could give credit to my senses.—
    [*Addressing the key.*] Thou dumb magician, that without a
        charm
    Did'st make my entrance easy, to possess   10
    What wise men wish and toil for. Hermes' moly,
    Sibylla's golden bough, the great elixir,

---

    199. *night-rail*] dressing-gown.
[III.iii]
    11. *Hermes' moly*] the herb given to Odysseus by Hermes (*Odyssey* x.
287–303) to protect him against the charms of Circe. (Cf. Milton, *Comus*,
ll. 636–637.)
    12. *Sibylla's golden bough*] which Aeneas plucked at the Sibyl's direction,
to present as a gift to Proserpine upon his descent into the underworld
(Virgil *Aeneid* vi. 136 ff.).

Imagin'd only by the alchemist,
Compar'd with thee are shadows, thou the substance
And guardian of felicity. No marvel,   15
My brother made thy place of rest his bosom,
Thou being the keeper of his heart, a mistress
To be hugg'd ever. In by-corners of
This sacred room, silver in bags heap'd up
Like billets saw'd, and ready for the fire,   20
Unworthy to hold fellowship with bright gold
That flow'd about the room, conceal'd itself.
There needs no artificial light; the splendor
Makes a perpetual day there, night and darkness
By that still-burning lamp forever banish'd.   25
But when, guided by that, my eyes had made
Discovery of the caskets, and they open'd,
Each sparkling diamond from itself shot forth
A pyramid of flames, and in the roof
Fix'd it a glorious star, and made the place   30
Heaven's abstract, or epitome: rubies, sapphires,
And ropes of orient pearl, these seen, I could not
But look on with contempt. And yet I found,
What weak credulity could have no faith in,
A treasure far exceeding these. Here lay   35
A manor bound fast in a skin of parchment,
The wax continuing hard, the acres melting.
Here a sure deed of gift for a market town,
If not redeem'd this day, which is not in
The unthrift's power: there being scarce one shire   40
In Wales or England, where my moneys are not
Lent out at usury, the certain hook
To draw in more. I am sublim'd! gross earth
Supports me not. I walk on air! —Who's there?
Thieves! raise the street! thieves!

Enter Lord [Lacy, *with*] Sir John [Frugal, Sir Maurice] Lacy, *and*
Plenty, *as Indians.*

LORD LACY.   What strange passion's this?   45

30. Fix'd] *Mason;* Fix *Q.*

---

40. *unthrift's*] prodigal's.

Have you your eyes? do you know me?

LUKE.   You, my lord,
　I do: but this retinue, in these shapes too,
　May well excuse my fears. When 'tis your pleasure
　That I should wait upon you, give me leave
　To do it at your own house, for I must tell you,   50
　Things as they now are with me, well consider'd,
　I do not like such visitants.

LORD LACY.   Yesterday
　When you had nothing, praise your poverty for't,
　You could have sung secure before a thief;
　But now you are grown rich, doubts and suspicions,   55
　And needless fears possess you. Thank a good brother,
　But let not this exalt you.

LUKE.   A good brother!
　Good in his conscience, I confess, and wise
　In giving o'er the world. But his estate,
　Which your lordship may conceive great, no way answers   60
　The general opinion. Alas,
　With a great charge, I am left a poor man by him.

LORD LACY.
　A poor man, say you?

LUKE.   Poor, compar'd with what
　'Tis thought I do possess. Some little land,
　Fair household furniture, a few good debts,   65
　But empty bags, I find: yet I will be
　A faithful steward to his wife and daughters,
　And to the utmost of my power obey
　His will in all things.

LORD LACY.   I'll not argue with you
　Of his estate, but bind you to performance   70
　Of his last request, which is, for testimony
　Of his religious charity, that you would
　Receive these Indians, lately sent him from
　Virginia, into your house; and labor
　At any rate with the best of your endeavors,   75
　Assisted by the aids of our divines,
　To make 'em Christians.

LUKE.   Call you this, my lord,

Religious charity? to send infidels,
Like hungry locusts, to devour the bread
Should feed his family? I neither can,   80
Nor will consent to 't.

LORD LACY.   Do not slight it; 'tis
With him a business of such consequence,
That should he only hear 'tis not embrac'd,
And cheerfully, in this his conscience aiming
At the saving of three souls, 'twill draw him o'er   85
To see it himself accomplish'd.

LUKE.   Heaven forbid
I should divert him from his holy purpose
To worldly cares again! I rather will
Sustain the burden, and with the converted
Feast the converters, who I know will prove   90
The greatest feeders.

SIR JOHN.
Oh, ha, enewah Chrish bully leika.

PLENTY.
Enaula.

SIR MAURICE.
Harrico botikia bonnery.

LUKE.
Ha! in this heathen language,   95
How is it possible our doctors should
Hold conference with 'em, or I use the means
For their conversion?

LORD LACY.   That shall be no hindrance
To your good purposes. They have liv'd long
In the English colony, and speak our language   100
As their own dialect; the business does concern you:
Mine own designs command me hence. Continue,
As in your poverty you were, a pious
And honest man.   *Exit.*

LUKE.   That is, interpreted,
A slave and beggar.

SIR JOHN.   You conceive it right,   105
There being no religion, nor virtue
But in abundance, and no vice but want.

All deities serve Plutus.

LUKE.   Oracle!

SIR JOHN.

Temples rais'd to ourselves in the increase
Of wealth and reputation, speak a wise man;   110
But sacrifice to an imagin'd power,
Of which we have no sense but in belief,
A superstitious fool.

LUKE.   True worldly wisdom!

SIR JOHN.

All knowledge else is folly.

SIR MAURICE.   Now we are yours,
Be confident your better angel is   115
Enter'd your house.

PLENTY.   There being nothing in
The compass of your wishes, but shall end
In their fruition to the full.

SIR JOHN.   As yet,
You do not know us, but when you understand
The wonders we can do, and what the ends were   120
That brought us hither, you will entertain us
With more respect.

LUKE [aside].   There's something whispers to me,
These are no common men. —My house is yours,
Enjoy it freely: only grant me this,
Not to be seen abroad till I have heard   125
More of your sacred principles. Pray enter.
You are learn'd Europeans, and we worse
Than ignorant Americans.

SIR JOHN.   You shall find it.   *Exeunt*

[IV.i]   *Enter* Ding'em, Gettall, *and* Holdfast.

DING'EM.

Not speak with him! with fear survey me better,
Thou figure of famine.

GETTALL.   Coming, as we do,

---

108. *Plutus*] the personification of wealth, son of Demeter and Iasion.

From his quondam patrons, his dear ingles now,
The brave spark Tradewell—

DING'EM.   And the man of men
In the service of a woman, gallant Goldwire!   5

                    Enter Luke.

HOLDFAST.
I know 'em for his prentices without
These flourishes. —[*To* Luke]. Here are rude fellows, sir.

DING'EM.
Not yours, you rascal!

HOLDFAST.   No, don pimp; you may seek 'em
In Bridewell, or the hole; here are none of your comrogues.

LUKE.
One of 'em looks as he would cut my throat: 10
Your business, friends?

HOLDFAST.   I'll fetch a constable;
Let him answer him in the stocks.

DING'EM   Stir and thou dar'st.
Fright me with Bridewell and the stocks! they are flea-bitings
I am familiar with.   [*Draws.*]

LUKE.   Pray you put up.—
[*To* Holdfast.] And sirrah, hold your peace.

DING'EM.   Thy word's a law,   15
And I obey. Live, scrape-shoe, and be thankful.
Thou man of muck and money, for as such
I now salute thee, the suburbian gamesters
Have heard thy fortunes, and I am in person
Sent to congratulate.

GETTALL.   The news hath reach'd   20
The ordinaries, and all the gamesters are
Ambitious to shake the golden golls

---

3. *ingles*] intimates.
8. *don*] in colloquial use, "a leader; an adept" (*OED*).
9. *Bridewell*] "a manor or house, so called—presented to the City of London by King Edward VI . . . as a Workhouse for the Poor, and a House of Correction 'for the strumpet and idle person, for the rioter that consumeth all, and for the vagabond that will abide in no place'" (Wheatley).
9. *the hole*] cf. I.i.36.   9. *comrogues*] fellow rogues.   12. *and*] if
16. *scrape-shoe*] "an obsequious person, a toady" (*OED*, conj.).
18. *suburbian*] cf. III.i.33.   22. *golls*] hands, or fists.

Of worshipful Master Luke. I come from Tradewell,
Your fine facetious factor.

DING'EM.   I from Goldwire:
He and his Helen have prepar'd a banquet,   25
With the appurtenances, to entertain thee,
For I must whisper in thine ear, thou art
To be her Paris; but bring money with thee
To quit old scores.

GETTALL.   Blind chance hath frown'd upon
Brave Tradewell. He's blown up, but not without   30
Hope of recovery, so you supply him
With a good round sum. In my house, I can assure you,
There's half a million stirring.

LUKE.   What hath he lost?

GETTALL.
Three hundred.

LUKE.   A trifle.

GETTALL.   Make it up a thousand,
And I will fit him with such tools as shall   35
Bring in a myriad.

LUKE.   They know me well,
Nor need you use such circumstances for 'em.
What's mine is theirs. They are my friends, not servants,
But in their care to enrich me, and these courses
The speeding means. Your name, I pray you?

GETTALL.   Gettall;   40
I have been many years an ordinary-keeper,
My box my poor revenue.

LUKE.   Your name suits well

---

24. *factor*] "one who buys or sells for another" (*OED*).

39. *But*] except.

39–40. *these . . . means*] these courses are the means they have taken to speed them to their end (of enriching me).

42. *My box my poor revenue*] If, in a dice game, "the caster throws three mains, or wins by throwing three times successively, he pays to the box-keeper, for the use of the house, a stipulated sum, varying according to the dignity of the place from eighteen pence to half a guinea. If the caster wins six times successively, he is requested, besides the usual payment to the house, to make a gratuitous donation to the box-keeper . . ." (*Monthly Mirror*, January, 1807, pp. 54–57, quoted by Kirk).

With your profession. Bid him bear up; he shall not
Sit long on penniless-bench.

GETTALL.   There spake an angel.

LUKE.

You know Mistress Shave'em?

GETTALL.   The pontifical punk?   45

LUKE.

The same. Let him meet me there some two hours hence,
And tell Tom Goldwire I will then be with him,
Furnish'd beyond his hopes; and let your mistress
Appear in her best trim.

DING'EM.   She will make thee young,
Old Aeson. She is ever furnish'd with   50
Medea's drugs, restoratives. I fly
To keep 'em sober till thy worship come;
They will be drunk with joy else.

GETTALL.   I'll run with you. *Exeunt* Ding'em *and* Gettall.

HOLDFAST.

You will not do as you say, I hope.

LUKE.   Inquire not;
I shall do what becomes me—To the door.

                        Knocking [within]. 55
New visitants: what are they?

HOLDFAST.   A whole batch, sir,
Almost of the same leaven: your needy debtors,
Penury, Fortune, Hoyst.

LUKE.   They come to gratulate
The fortune fall'n upon me.

HOLDFAST.   Rather, sir,
Like the others, to prey on you.

LUKE.   I am simple;   60
They know my good nature. But let 'em in however.

HOLDFAST

All will come to ruin! I see beggary
Already knocking at the door. —You may enter:
But use a conscience, and do not work upon

---

44. *penniless-bench*] "A cant term for a state of poverty" (Nares).
50. *Old Aeson*] Jason's father, restored to youth by Medea's magic.

A tenderhearted gentleman too much;   65
'Twill show like charity in you.

       Enter Fortune, Penury, *and* Hoyst.

LUKE.   Welcome, friends:
I know your hearts and wishes; you are glad
You have chang'd your creditor.
PENURY.   I weep for joy
To look upon his worship's face.
FORTUNE.   His worship's!
I see lord mayor written on his forehead;   70
The cap of maintenance, and city sword
Borne up in state before him.
HOYST.   Hospitals,
And a third Burse erected by his honor.
PENURY.
The city poet on the pageant day
Preferring him before Gresham.
HOYST.   All the conduits   75
Spouting canary sack.
FORTUNE.   Not a prisoner left,
Under ten pounds.
PENURY.   We his poor beadsmen feasting
Our neighbors on his bounty.
LUKE.   May I make good
Your prophecies, gentle friends, as I'll endeavor
To the utmost of my power.
HOLDFAST.   Yes, for one year,   80
And break the next.
LUKE.   You are ever prating, sirrah.

---

70. mayor] *Coxeter;* Major *Q.*

---

71. *cap of maintenance, and city sword*] symbols of official dignity, borne
before the Lord Mayor, and before the sovereign at his coronation.

73. *a third Burse*] cf. notes on I.i.128 and III.i.13.

75. *Gresham*] Thomas Gresham (1519?–1579), founder of the Royal
Exchange. (Cf. note on I.i.128.)

76–77. *Not . . . pounds*] all who have been imprisoned for debts amounting
to less than ten pounds having been released through Luke's presumed
benevolence.

77. *beadsmen*] cf. I.iii.101.

Your present business, friends?

FORTUNE.   Were your brother present,
Mine had been of some consequence; but now
The power lies in your worship's hand, 'tis little,
And will I know, as soon as ask'd, be granted.   85

LUKE.
'Tis very probable.

FORTUNE.   The kind forbearance
Of my great debt, by your means, heav'n prais'd for't,
Hath rais'd my sunk estate. I have two ships,
Which I long since gave lost, above my hopes
Return'd from Barbary, and richly freighted.   90

LUKE.
Where are they?

FORTUNE.   Near Gravesend.

LUKE.   I am truly glad of 't.

FORTUNE.
I find your worship's charity, and dare swear so.
Now may I have your license, as I know
With willingness I shall, to make the best
Of the commodities—though you have execution,   95
And after judgment against all that's mine,
As my poor body—I shall be enabl'd
To make payment of my debts to all the world,
And leave myself a competence.

LUKE.   You much wrong me,
If you only doubt it. Yours, Master Hoyst?   100

HOYST.
'Tis the surrend'ring back the mortgage of
My lands, and on good terms, but three days patience;
By an uncle's death I have means left to redeem it,
And cancel all the forfeited bonds I seal'd to
In my riots to the merchant, for I am   105

---

91. *Gravesend*] a port in Kent on the south bank of the Thames, thirty miles below London.

95–96. *execution . . . judgment*] "execution" is short for Writ of Execution: "the process under which the sheriff is commanded to execute a judgment" (*OED*).

99. *competence*] "a sufficiency of means for living comfortably" (*OED*).

Resolv'd to leave off play, and turn good husband.

LUKE.

A good intent, and to be cherish'd in you.
Yours, Penury?

PENURY.   My state stands as it did, sir:
What I ow'd I owe, but can pay nothing to you.
Yet if you please to trust me with ten pounds more,   110
I can buy a commodity of a sailor
Will make me a freeman. There, sir, is his name;
And the parcels I am to deal for.   *Gives him a paper.*

LUKE.   You are all so reasonable
In your demands, that I must freely grant 'em.
Some three hours hence meet me on the Exchange,   115
You shall be amply satisfied.

PENURY.   Heaven preserve you.

FORTUNE.

Happy were London if within her walls
She had many such rich men.

LUKE.   No more, now leave me;
                    Exeunt Fortune, Hoyst, *and* Penury.
I am full of various thoughts. Be careful, Holdfast,
I have much to do.

HOLDFAST.   And I something to say,   120
Would you give me hearing.

LUKE.   At my better leisure.
'Till my return, look well unto the Indians.
In the meantime, do you as this directs you.
                    [*Gives him a paper.*] *Exeunt.*

[IV.ii]
Enter [Young] Goldwire, [Young] Tradewell, Shave'em, Secret,
Gettall, *and* Ding'em.

YOUNG GOLDWIRE.

"All that is mine is theirs." Those were his words?

DING'EM.

I am authentical.

YOUNG TRADEWELL.   And that I should not

---

106. *turn good husband*] i.e., manage with thrift and prudence.

Sit long on penniless-bench?

GETTALL.   But suddenly start up
A gamester at the height, and cry "At all!"

SHAVE'EM.

And did he seem to have an inclination   5
To toy with me?

DING'EM.   He wish'd you would put on
Your best habiliments, for he resolv'd
To make a jovial day on't.

YOUNG GOLDWIRE.   Hug him close, wench,
And thou may'st eat gold and amber. I well know him
For a most insatiate drabber. He hath given,   10
Before he spent his own estate, which was
Nothing to the huge mass he's now possess'd of,
A hundred pound a leap.

SHAVE'EM.   Hell take my doctor!
He should have brought me some fresh oil of talc;
These ceruses are common.

SECRET.   'Troth, sweet lady,   15
The colors are well laid on.

YOUNG GOLDWIRE.   And thick enough;
I find that on my lips.

SHAVE'EM.   Do you so, Jack Sauce!
I'll keep 'em further off.

YOUNG GOLDWIRE.   But be assur'd first
Of a new maintainer e'er you cashier the old one.
But bind him fast by thy sorceries, and thou shalt   20
Be my revenue; the whole college study
The reparation of thy ruin'd face;
Thou shalt have thy proper and baldheaded coachman;
Thy tailor and embroiderer shall kneel

---

4. *"At all!"*] "If the caster is full of cash and spirit, it is usual for him to say 'at all in the ring,' meaning that he will play for any sums all the company may choose to risk against him. To this bold style of play, Gettall, the box-keeper, alludes" (*Monthly Mirror*, January, 1807, pp. 54–57, quoted by Kirk). Cf. IV.i.42, note.

10. *drabber*] a follower of loose women.

14. *oil of talc*] "A preparative formerly used as a cosmetic" (*OED*).

15. *ceruse*] white lead, used as a paint or cosmetic.

21. *college*] i.e., of doctors (cf. line 13).

To thee, their idol. Cheapside and the Exchange   25
Shall court thy custom, and thou shalt forget
There ever was a St. Martin's. Thy procurer
Shall be sheath'd in velvet, and a reverend veil
Pass her for a grave matron. Have an eye to the door,
And let loud music when this monarch enters   30
Proclaim his entertainment.

DING'EM.   That's my office.   *Cornets flourish.*
The consort's ready.

Enter Luke.

YOUNG TRADEWELL.   And the god of pleasure,
Master Luke our Comus, enters.
YOUNG GOLDWIRE.   Set your face in order,
I will prepare him. —Live I to see this day,
And to acknowledge you my royal master?   35
YOUNG TRADEWELL.
Let the iron chests fly open, and the gold,
Rusty for want of use, appear again!
GETTALL.
Make my ordinary flourish!
SHAVE'EM.   Welcome, sir,
To your own palace.   *Music.*
YOUNG GOLDWIRE.   Kiss your Cleopatra,
And show yourself in your magnificent bounties   40
A second Anthony!
DING'EM.   All the nine worthies!

---

25. *Cheapside*] the old market place of London; "a street between the
Poultry and St. Paul's, a portion of the line from Charing Cross to the
Royal Exchange, and from Holborn to the Bank of England" (Wheatley).
27. *St. Martin's*] the collegiate church of St. Martin's-le-Grand. Though
the church was destroyed at the dissolution of the monasteries in the reign
of Henry VIII, the privileges of sanctuary remained till 1697, with the
result that the surrounding region became the resort of all manner of
criminals and debtors, who were there exempt from arrest.
32. *consort*] company of musicians.
33. *Comus*] son of Bacchus and Circe.
38. *Make . . . flourish*] cf. IV.i. 41–42, and I.iii.7, note.

SECRET.

    Variety of pleasures wait on you,
    And a strong back!

LUKE.   Give me leave to breathe, I pray you.

    I am astonish'd! All this preparation
    For me? and this choice modest beauty wrought   45
    To feed my appetite?

ALL.   We are all your creatures.

LUKE.

    A house well furnish'd!

YOUNG GOLDWIRE.   At your own cost, sir,

    Glad I the instrument. I prophesied
    You should possess what now you do, and therefore
    Prepar'd it for your pleasure. There's no rag   50
    This Venus wears, but on my knowledge was
    Deriv'd from your brother's cash. The lease of the house
    And furniture, cost near a thousand, sir.

SHAVE'EM.

    But now you are master both of it and me,
    I hope you'll build elsewhere.

LUKE.   And see you plac'd,   55

    Fair one, to your desert. As I live, friend Tradewell,
    I hardly knew you, your clothes so well become you.
    What is your loss? speak truth.

YOUNG TRADEWELL.   Three hundred, sir.

GETTALL.

    But on a new supply he shall recover
    The sum told twenty times o'er.

SHAVE'EM.   There is a banket,   60

    And after that a soft couch that attends you.

LUKE.

    I couple not in the daylight. Expectation
    Heightens the pleasure of the night, my sweet one.
    Your music's harsh, discharge it. I have provided
    A better consort, and you shall frolic it   65
    In another place.   *Cease music.*

YOUNG GOLDWIRE.   But have you brought gold, and store, sir?

---

60. *banket*] banquet.
66. *But . . . sir?*] "a line from an old ballad" (Gifford).

YOUNG TRADEWELL.
I long to "Ware the caster!"

YOUNG GOLDWIRE.   I to appear
In a fresh habit.

SHAVE'EM.   My mercer and my silkman
Waited me two hours since.

LUKE.   I am no porter,
To carry so much gold as will supply   70
Your vast desires, but I have ta'en order for you;

Enter Sheriff, Marshal, *and officers.*

You shall have what is fitting, and they come here
Will see it perform'd. —Do your offices: you have
My lord chief justice's warrant for't.

SHERIFF.   Seize 'em all.

SHAVE'EM.
The city marshal!

YOUNG GOLDWIRE.   And the sheriff! I know him.   75

SECRET.
We are betray'd.

DING'EM.   Undone.

GETTALL.   Dear Master Luke.

YOUNG GOLDWIRE.
You cannot be so cruel. Your persuasion
Chid us into these courses, oft repeating,
"Show yourselves city-sparks, and hang up money."

LUKE.
True, when it was my brother's I contemn'd it,   80
But now it is mine own, the case is alter'd.

---

67. *"Ware the caster!"*] "... when a setter supposes himself to possess
more money than the caster, it is usual for him on putting his stake in the
ring to cry 'ware caster.' The caster then declares, at all under such or
such a sum, ten, twenty, or fifty pounds, for instance, or else to place against
the stakes of certain setters the corresponding sums, and cry 'ware cover'd
only.' Thus, then, in two phrases, the city prodigal [Tradewell] expresses
his hope that the supply of money he expects will enable him to be lord-
paramount of the gaming table: as caster to be *at all* [cf. IV.ii.4, and note];
and as setter to 'ware the caster'" (*Monthly Mirror*, January, 1807, pp.
54–57, quoted by Kirk, p. 165). See also IV.i.42, note.

YOUNG TRADEWELL.
>Will you prove yourself a devil? tempt us to mischief,
>And then discover it?

LUKE.   Argue that hereafter.
>In the meantime, Master Goldwire, you that made
>Your ten-pound suppers; kept your punks at livery   85
>In Brainford, Staines, and Barnet, and this in London;
>Held correspondence with your fellow cashiers,
>Ka me, ka thee; and knew in your accompts
>To cheat my brother—if you can, evade me.
>If there be law in London your fathers' bonds   90
>Shall answer for what you are out.

YOUNG GOLDWIRE.   You often told us
>It was a bugbear.

LUKE.   Such a one as shall fright 'em
>Out of their estates to make me satisfaction
>To the utmost scruple. And for you, madam,
>My Cleopatra, by your own confession   95
>Your house, and all your movables, are mine;
>Nor shall you nor your matron need to trouble
>Your mercer, or your silkman; a blue gown,
>And a whip to boot, as I will handle it,
>Will serve the turn in Bridewell; and these soft hands,   100
>When they are inur'd to beating hemp, be scour'd
>In your penitent tears, and quite forget
>Powders and bitter almonds.

SHAVE'EM, SECRET, DING'EM.   Will you show no mercy?

LUKE.
>I am inexorable.

GETTALL.   I'll make bold
>To take my leave; the gamesters stay my coming.   105

LUKE.
>We must not part so, gentle Master Gettall.

---

98. *a blue gown*] "the dress of ignominy for a harlot in the house of correction" (Nares).

101. *beating hemp*] "Sir Thomas Myddleton, president of Bridewell from 1613 to 1631, set professional beggars to work beating hemp on the blocks" (Kirk).

Your box, your certain income, must pay back
Three hundred, as I take it, or you lie by it.
There's half a million stirring in your house,
This a poor trifle. —Master Shriefe and Master Marshal,   110
On your perils do your offices.

YOUNG GOLDWIRE [*to* Young Tradewell].   Dost thou cry now
Like a maudlin gamester after loss? I'll suffer
Like a boman, and now in my misery,
In scorn of all thy wealth, to thy teeth tell thee
Thou wert my pander.

LUKE.   Shall I hear this from   115
My prentice?

MARSHAL.   Stop his mouth.

SHERIFF.   Away with 'em.   *Exeunt* Sheriff, Marshal, *and the rest.*

LUKE.
A prosperous omen in my entrance to
My alter'd nature! These house thieves remov'd,
And what was lost, beyond my hopes recover'd,
Will add unto my heap. Increase of wealth   120
Is the rich man's ambition, and mine
Shall know no bounds. The valiant Macedon,
Having in his conceit subdu'd one world,
Lamented that there were no more to conquer:
In my way, he shall be my great example.   125
And when my private house in cramm'd abundance
Shall prove the chamber of the city poor,
And Genoway's bankers shall look pale with envy
When I am mention'd, I shall grieve there is
No more to be exhausted in one kingdom.   130
Religion, conscience, charity, farewell!
To me you are words only, and no more;
All human happiness consists in store.   *Exit.*

---

108. *lie by it*] i.e., lie in prison.
110. *Shriefe*] sheriff.
113. *boman*] a slang term for a gallant fellow.
122. *valiant Macedon*] Alexander the Great.
128. *Genoway's*] Genoa's.
133. *store*] abundance.

[IV.iii]   *Enter* Sergeants, Fortune, Hoyst, Penury.

FORTUNE.
    At Master Luke's suit? the action twenty thousand?
1 SERGEANT.
    With two or three executions, which shall grind you
    To powder when we have you in the Counter.
FORTUNE.
    Thou dost belie him, varlet. He, good gentleman,
    Will weep when he hears how we are us'd.
1 SERGEANT.   Yes, millstones.   5
PENURY.
    He promis'd to lend me ten pound for a bargain,
    He will not do it this way.
2 SERGEANT.   I have warrant
    For what I have done. You are a poor fellow,
    And there being little to be got by you,
    In charity, as I am an officer,   10
    I would not have seen you, but upon compulsion,
    And for mine own security.
3 SERGEANT.   You are a gallant,
    And I do you a courtesy; provided
    That you have money. For a piece an hour
    I'll keep you in the house, till you send for bail.   15
2 SERGEANT.
    In the meantime, yeoman, run to the other Counter,
    And search if there be ought else out against him.
3 SERGEANT.
    That done, haste to his creditors. He's a prize,
    And as we are city pirates by our oaths,
    We must make the best on't.
HOYST.   Do your worst, I care not.   20
    I'll be remov'd to the Fleet, and drink and drab there
    In spite of your teeth. I now repent I ever
    Intended to be honest.

---

16. *the other Counter*] cf. I.i.35, note.
21. *the Fleet*] a London prison. Fleet Marriages, performed by any clergyman who might be confined there for debt, were notorious in the seventeenth century.

Enter Luke.

3 SERGEANT.   Here he comes
    You had best tell so.
FORTUNE.   Worshipful sir,
    You come in time to free us from these bandogs.   25
    I know you gave no way to't.
PENURY.   Or if you did,
    'Twas but to try our patience.
HOYST.   I must tell you
    I do not like such trials.
LUKE.   Are you sergeants
    Acquainted with the danger of a rescue,
    Yet stand here prating in the street? The Counter   30
    Is a safer place to parley in.
FORTUNE.   Are you in earnest?
LUKE.
    Yes faith, I will be satisfied to a token,
    Or build upon't you rot there.
FORTUNE.   Can a gentleman
    Of your soft and silken temper, speak such language?
PENURY.
    So honest, so religious?
HOYST.   That preach'd   35
    So much of charity for us to your brother?
LUKE.
    Yes, when I was in poverty it show'd well;
    But I inherit with his state, his mind,
    And rougher nature. I grant, then I talk'd
    For some ends to myself conceal'd, of pity,   40
    The poor man's orisons; and such like nothing.
    But what I thought, you all shall feel, and with rigor.
    Kind Master Luke says it. —[*To the Sergeants.*] Who pays
       for your attendance?
    Do you wait gratis?

---

    25. *bandogs*] "Properly *band-dog*, or bound-dog. A dog always kept tied
up on account of his fierceness" (Nares). Hence, generally mastiffs, blood-
hounds.
    33. *build upon't*] depend upon it.

FORTUNE.   Hear us speak.
LUKE.   While I,
    Like the adder, stop mine ears. Or did I listen,   45
    Though you spake with the tongues of angels to me,
    I am not to be alter'd.
FORTUNE.   Let me make the best
    Of my ships, and their freight.
PENURY.
    Lend me the ten pounds you promis'd.
HOYST.
    A day or two's patience to redeem my mortgage,   50
    And you shall be satisfied.
FORTUNE.   To the utmost farthing.
LUKE.
    I'll show some mercy; which is, that I will not
    Torture you with false hopes, but make you know
    What you shall trust to. —[To Fortune.] Your ships to my
        use
    Are seized on. —[To Penury.] I have got into my hands   55
    Your bargains from the sailor, 'twas a good one
    For such a petty sum. —[To Hoyst.] I will likewise take
    The extremity of your mortgage, and the forfeit
    Of your several bonds; the use and principal
    Shall not serve. —Think of the basket, wretches,   60
    And a coal sack for a winding-sheet.
FORTUNE.
    Broker!
HOYST.   Jew!
FORTUNE.   Imposer!
HOYST.   Cutthroat!
FORTUNE.   Hypocrite!
LUKE.
    Do, rail on.

---

45. *Like . . . ears*] adders were traditionally said to be deaf. Cf. Psalms
58:4.
    58. *extremity*] utmost degree.
    59. *use*] interest.
    60. *basket*] cf. I.i.114, note.
    62. *Imposer*] impostor.

Move mountains with your breath, it shakes not me.

PENURY.

    On my knees I beg compassion. My wife and children   65
    Shall hourly pray for your worship.

FORTUNE.   Mine betake thee
    To the devil thy tutor.

PENURY.   Look upon my tears.

HOYST.

    My rage.

FORTUNE.   My wrongs.

LUKE.   They are all alike to me:
    Intreats, curses, prayers, or imprecations.
    Do your duties, sergeants, I am elsewhere look'd for.   70

                                   Exit Luke.

3 SERGEANT.

    This your kind creditor?

2 SERGEANT.   A vast villain, rather.

PENURY.

    See, see, the sergeants pity us. Yet he's marble.

HOYST.

    Buried alive!

FORTUNE.   There's no means to avoid it.   *Exeunt.*

[IV.iv]   *Enter* Holdfast, Stargaze, *and* Milliscent.

STARGAZE.

    Not wait upon my lady?

HOLDFAST.   Nor come at her;
    You find it not in your almanac.

MILLISCENT.   Nor I have license
    To bring her breakfast.

HOLDFAST.   My new master hath
    Decreed this for a fasting day. She hath feasted long,
    And after a carnival, Lent ever follows.   5

MILLISCENT.

    Give me the key of her wardrobe. You'll repent this:
    I must know what gown she'll wear.

HOLDFAST.   You are mistaken,
    Dame president of the sweetmeats. She and her daughters
    Are turn'd philosophers, and must carry all

Their wealth about 'em. They have clothes laid in their
    chamber,   10
If they please to put 'em on, and without help too,
Or they may walk naked. You look, Master Stargaze,
As you had seen a strange comet, and had now foretold,
The end of the world, and on what day. And you,
As the wasps had broke into the gallipots,   15
And eaten up your apricots.

(*Within*) LADY FRUGAL.   Stargazer! Milliscent!

MILLISCENT.
    My lady's voice.

HOLDFAST.   Stir not, you are confin'd here.—
Your ladyship may approach them if you please,
But they are bound in this circle.

(*Within*) LADY FRUGAL.   Mine own bees
Rebel against me! When my kind brother knows this   20
I will be so reveng'd—

HOLDFAST.   The world's well alter'd.
He's your kind brother now, but yesterday
Your slave and jesting-stock.

    Enter Lady [Frugal], Anne, Mary, *in coarse habit, weeping.*

MILLISCENT.   What witch hath transform'd you?

STARGAZE.
    Is this the glorious shape your cheating brother
    Promis'd you should appear in?

MILLISCENT.   My young ladies   25
    In buffin gowns, and green aprons! tear 'em off,
    Rather show all than be seen thus.

HOLDFAST.   'Tis more comely,
    Iwis, than their other whim-whams.

MILLISCENT.   A French hood too;
    Now 'tis out of fashion, a fool's cap would show better.

---

15. *gallipots*] small earthen glazed pots.
26. *buffin*] a coarse cloth, used in gowns for the middle classes.
28. *Iwis*] certainly.
28. *French hood*] "a form of hood worn by women in the sixteenth and
seventeenth centuries having the front depressed over the forehead and
raised in folds or loops over the temples" (*OED*).

LADY FRUGAL.
> We are fool'd indeed! By whose command are we us'd thus?   30

Enter Luke.

HOLDFAST.
> Here he comes that can best resolve you.

LADY FRUGAL.   O good brother!
> Do you thus preserve your protestation to me?
> Can queens envy this habit? or did Juno
> E'er feast in such a shape?

ANNE.   You talk'd of Hebe,
> Of Iris, and I know not what; but were they   35
> Dress'd as we are, they were sure some chandler's daughters
> Bleaching linen in Moorfields.

MARY.   Or Exchange-wenches,
> Coming from eating pudding-pies on a Sunday
> At Pimlico, or Islington.

LUKE.   Save you, sister.
> I now dare style you so: you were before   40
> Too glorious to be look'd on; now you appear
> Like a city matron, and my pretty nieces
> Such things as were born and bred there. Why should you ape
> The fashions of court ladies, whose high titles,
> And pedigrees of long descent, give warrant   45
> For their superfluous bravery? 'twas monstrous:
> Till now you ne'er look'd lovely.

LADY FRUGAL.   Is this spoken
> In scorn?

LUKE.   Fie, no! with judgment. I make good
> My promise, and now show you like yourselves,
> In your own natural shapes, and stand resolv'd   50
> You shall continue so.

---

39. *Pimlico*] "near Hoxton, a great summer resort in the early part of the
seventeenth century, and famed for its cakes, custards and Derby ale"
(Wheatley).

39. *Islington*] in the seventeenth century, a country village to the north
of London, famous for its "houses of entertainment with their tea-gardens
and ducking-ponds, cheesecakes and custards, and fields, the favourite
Sunday resort of rural-minded citizens" (Wheatley).

39. *Save you*] may God save you.   46. *bravery*] cf. I.i.24.

LADY FRUGAL.   It is confess'd, sir.

LUKE.

Sir! Sirrah. Use your old phrase, I can bear it.

LADY FRUGAL.

That, if you please, forgotten. We acknowledge
We have deserv'd ill from you, yet despair not;
Though we are at your disposure, you'll maintain us   55
Like your brother's wife and daughters.

LUKE.   'Tis my purpose.

LADY FRUGAL.

And not make us ridiculous.

LUKE.   Admir'd rather,
As fair examples for our proud city dames,
And their proud brood to imitate. Do not frown;
If you do, I laugh, and glory that I have   60
The power, in you, to scourge a general vice,
And rise up a new satirist. But hear gently,
And in a gentle phrase I'll reprehend
Your late disguis'd deformity, and cry up
This decency and neatness, with th' advantage   65
You shall receive by't.

LADY FRUGAL.   We are bound to hear you.

LUKE.

With a soul inclin'd to learn. Your father was
An honest country farmer, Goodman Humble,
By his neighbors ne'er call'd Master. Did your pride
Descend from him? but let that pass. Your fortune,   70
Or rather your husband's industry, advanc'd you
To the rank of a merchant's wife. He made a knight,
And your sweet mistress-ship ladyfied, you wore
Satin on solemn days, a chain of gold,
A velvet hood, rich borders, and sometimes   75
A dainty miniver cap, a silver pin
Headed with a pearl worth threepence, and thus far
You were privileg'd, and no man envied it;
It being for the city's honor, that
There should be a distinction between   80

---

76. *miniver*] "the furre of Ermines mixed, or spotted, with the furre of the
Weesell" (Cotgrave).

The wife of a patrician, and plebeian.

MILLISCENT.

    Pray you, leave preaching, or choose some other text;
    Your rhetoric is too moving, for it makes
    Your auditory weep.

LUKE.   Peace, chattering magpie,
    I'll treat of you anon. —But when the height   85
    And dignity of London's blessings grew
    Contemptible, and the name lady mayoress
    Became a byword, and you scorn'd the means
    By which you were rais'd, my brother's fond indulgence
    Giving the reins to't; and no object pleas'd you   90
    But the glittering pomp and bravery of the court:
    What a strange, nay monstrous metamorphosis follow'd!
    No English workman then could please your fancy;
    The French and Tuscan dress your whole discourse;
    This bawd to prodigality entertain'd   95
    To buzz into your ears what shape this countess
    Appear'd in the last masque, and how it drew
    The young lords' eyes upon her; and this usher
    Succeeded in the eldest prentice's place
    To walk before you.

LADY FRUGAL.   Pray you, end.

HOLDFAST.   Proceed, sir;   100
    I could fast almost a prenticeship to hear you,
    You touch 'em so to the quick.

LUKE.   Then as I said,
    The reverend hood cast off, your borrow'd hair
    Powder'd and curl'd, was by your dresser's art
    Form'd like a coronet, hang'd with diamonds,   105
    And the richest orient pearl; your carcanets
    That did adorn your neck of equal value;
    Your Hungerland bands, and Spanish quellio ruffs;

---

   101. *fast . . . prenticeship*] i.e., for seven years, the usual term for which an apprentice was bound to the service of his master.

   106. *carcanets*] necklaces.

   108. *Hungerland bands*] presumably of an Hungarian style. The fashion has not been identified.

   108. *quellio ruffs*] "Supposed to be put for cuello, which is Spanish for a collar" (Nares).

Great lords and ladies feasted to survey
Embroider'd petticoats; and sickness feign'd　　　　　　110
That your night-rails of forty pounds apiece
Might be seen with envy of the visitants;
Rich pantables in ostentation shown,
And roses worth a family; you were serv'd in plate;
Stirr'd not a foot without your coach. And going　　　115
To church not for devotion, but to show
Your pomp, you were tickl'd when the beggars cried,
"Heaven save your honor!" This idolatry
Paid to a painted room.

HOLDFAST.　　　　　　　　Nay, you have reason
To blubber, all of you.

LUKE.　　　　　　　　And when you lay　　　　　120
In childbed, at the christ'ning of this minx,
I well remember it, as you had been
An absolute princess, since they have no more,
Three several chambers hung. The first with arras,
And that for waiters; the second crimson satin,　　　125
For the meaner sort of guests; the third of scarlet,
Of the rich Tyrian dye; a canopy
To cover the brat's cradle; you in state
Like Pompey's Julia.

LADY FRUGAL.　　　　　　No more, I pray you.

LUKE.

Of this be sure you shall not. I'll cut off　　　　　130
Whatever is exorbitant in you,
Or in your daughters, and reduce you to
Your natural forms and habits; not in revenge
Of your base usage of me, but to fright

131–138.] Q contains marginal S.D.　　step, little/ Table, and/ Arras hung/ up
"Whil'st the/ Act Plays,/ the Foot-/　　for the/ Musicians."

113. pantables] cf. III.i.96.　　114. roses] cf. I.i.105. S.D.
123. since ... more] since princesses have no more luxuries than you
indulged in.
124. several] different.
124. arras] "A rich tapestry fabric, in which figures and scenes are woven
in colors" (OED).
127. Tyrian dye] "the purple or crimson dye anciently made at Tyre
from certain molluscs" (OED).
129. Julia] wife of Pompey the Great, and daughter of Julius Caesar.

Others by your example. 'Tis decreed   135
You shall serve one another, for I will
Allow no waiter to you. Out of doors
With these useless drones!

HOLDFAST.   Will you pack?

MILLISCENT.   Not till I have
My trunks along with me.

LUKE.   Not a rag! you came
Hither without a box.

STARGAZE.   You'll show to me,   140
I hope, sir, more compassion.

HOLDFAST.   Troth I'll be
Thus far a suitor for him. He hath printed
An almanac for this year at his own charge;
Let him have th' impression with him to set up with.

LUKE.
For once I'll be entreated. Let it be   145
Thrown to him out of the window.

STARGAZE.   O cursed stars
That reign'd at my nativity! how have you cheated
Your poor observer.

ANNE.   Must we part in tears?

MARY.
Farewell, good Milliscent.

LADY FRUGAL.   I am sick, and meet with
A rough physician. O my pride and scorn!   150
How justly am I punish'd!

MARY.   Now we suffer
For our stubbornness and disobedience
To our good father.

ANNE.   And the base conditions
We impos'd upon our suitors.

LUKE.   Get you in,
And caterwaul in a corner.

LADY FRUGAL.   There's no contending.   155

Lady [Frugal], Anne, Mary, *go off at one door;* Stargaze *and* Milliscent
at the other.

---

155. *caterwaul*] "to make a discordant, hideous noise; to quarrel like
cats" (*OED*).

LUKE.
How lik'st thou my carriage, Holdfast?

HOLDFAST.   Well in some part,
But it relishes I know not how, a little
Of too much tyranny.

LUKE.   Thou art a fool.
He's cruel to himself, that dares not be
Severe to those that us'd him cruelly.   *Exeunt.* 160

[V.i]

Enter Luke, [*with*] Sir John [Frugal, Sir Maurice], Lacy, *and* Plenty
[*in their Indian disguise*].

LUKE.
You care not then, as it seems, to be converted
To our religion.

SIR JOHN.   We know no such word,
Nor power but the devil, and him we serve for fear,
Not love.

LUKE.   I am glad that charge is sav'd.

SIR JOHN.   We put
That trick upon your brother, to have means   5
To come to the city. Now to you we'll discover
The close design that brought us, with assurance
If you lend your aids to furnish us with that
Which in the colony was not to be purchas'd,
No merchant ever made such a return   10
For his most precious venture, as you shall
Receive from us; far, far above your hopes,
Or fancy to imagine.

LUKE.   It must be
Some strange commodity, and of a dear value,
(Such an opinion is planted in me   15

7–11.] *Q contains marginal S.D.   for the song/ at Aras."*
"Musicians/ come down to/ make ready/

---

7. *close*] secret.

You will deal fairly) that I would not hazard.
Give me the name of't.

SIR MAURICE.   I fear you will make
Some scruple in your conscience to grant it.

LUKE.
Conscience! No, no; so it may be done with safety,
And without danger of the law.

PLENTY.   For that   20
You shall sleep securely. Nor shall it diminish,
But add unto your heap such an increase,
As what you now possess shall appear an atom
To the mountain it brings with it.

LUKE.   Do not rack me
With expectation.

SIR JOHN.   Thus then in a word: 25
The devil— Why start you at his name? If you
Desire to wallow in wealth and wordly honors,
You must make haste to be familiar with him.
This devil, whose priest I am, and by him made
A deep magician (for I can do wonders),   30
Appear'd to me in Virginia, and commanded
With many stripes (for that's his cruel custom)
I should provide on pain of his fierce wrath
Against the next great sacrifice, at which
We, groveling on our faces, fall before him,   35
Two Christian virgins, that with their pure blood
Might dye his horrid altars, and a third
(In his hate to such embraces as are lawful)
Married, and with your ceremonious rites,
As an oblation unto Hecate,   40
And wanton Lust, her favorite.

LUKE.   A devilish custom:
And yet why should it startle me? There are
Enough of the sex fit for this use; but virgins,
And such a matron as you speak of, hardly

---

30. *deep*] "profound in craft or subtlety" (Onions).
32. *stripes*] blows, lashes.
40. *Hecate*] a Greek goddess, associated with the moon, the night, and the lower world, and regarded as the protectress of enchanters and witches.

To be wrought to it.

PLENTY.   A mine of gold for a fee   45
Waits him that undertakes it, and performs it.

SIR MAURICE.
Know you no distressed widow, or poor maids,
Whose want of dower, though well born, makes 'em weary
Of their own country?

SIR JOHN.   Such as had rather be
Miserable in another world, than where   50
They have surfeited in felicity?

LUKE.   Give me leave.—
[*Aside.*] I would not lose this purchase. A grave matron!
And two pure virgins. Umph! I think my sister,
Though proud, was ever honest; and my nieces
Untainted yet. Why should not they be shipp'd   55
For this employment? They are burdensome to me,
And eat too much. And if they stay in London,
They will find friends that to my loss will force me
To composition. 'Twere a masterpiece
If this could be effected. They were ever   60
Ambitious of title. Should I urge,
Matching with these, they shall live Indian queens,
It may do much. But what shall I feel here,
Knowing to what they are design'd? They absent,
The thought of them will leave me. It shall be so.   65
—I'll furnish you, and to endear the service,
In mine own family, and my blood too.

SIR JOHN.
Make this good, and your house shall not contain
The gold we'll send you.

LUKE.   You have seen my sister,
And my two nieces?

SIR JOHN.   Yes, sir.

LUKE.   These persuaded   70
How happily they shall live, and in what pomp
When they are in your kingdoms, for you must

---

54. *honest*] virtuous.
59. *composition*] "an agreement or arrangement involving surrender or
sacrifice of some kind on one side or on both" (*OED*).

Work 'em a belief that you are kings—
PLENTY.   We are so.
LUKE.
    I'll put it in practice instantly. Study you
    For moving language. —Sister! Nieces!

Enter Lady [Frugal], Anne, Mary.

                     How!   75
    Still mourning? Dry your eyes, and clear these clouds
    That do obscure your beauties. Did you believe
    My personated reprehension, though
    It show'd like a rough anger, could be serious?
    Forget the fright I put you in. My ends   80
    In humbling you was to set off the height
    Of honor, principal honor, which my studies
    When you least expect it shall confer upon you.
    Still you seem doubtful: be not wanting to
    Yourselves, nor let the strangeness of the means,   85
    With the shadow of some danger, render you
    Incredulous.
LADY FRUGAL.   Our usage hath been such,
    As we can faintly hope that your intents
    And language are the same.
LUKE.   I'll change those hopes
    To certainties.
SIR JOHN [*aside*].   With what art he winds about them!   90
LUKE.
    What will you say, or what thanks shall I look for,
    If now I raise you to such eminence as
    The wife and daughters of a citizen
    Never arriv'd at? Many for their wealth, I grant,
    Have written ladies of honor, and some few   95
    Have higher titles, and that's the farthest rise
    You can in England hope for. What think you
    If I should mark you out a way to live
    Queens in another climate?

95–98.] *Q contains marginal S.D.   Wine."*
"The Banquet/ ready. One/ Chair, and/

ANNE. We desire
A competence.

MARY. And prefer our country's smoke 100
Before outlandish fire.

LADY FRUGAL. But should we listen
To such impossibilities, 'tis not in
The power of man to make it good.

LUKE. I'll do't;
Nor is this seat of majesty far remov'd.
It is but to Virginia.

LADY FRUGAL. How! Virginia! 105
High heaven forbid! Remember, sir, I beseech you,
What creatures are shipp'd thither.

ANNE. Condemn'd wretches,
Forfeited to the law.

MARY. Strumpets and bawds,
For the abomination of their life,
Spew'd out of their own country.

LUKE. Your false fears 110
Abuse my noble purpose. Such indeed
Are sent as slaves to labor there, but you
To absolute sovereignty. Observe these men,
With reverence observe them. They are kings,
Kings of such spacious territories and dominions, 115
As our great Britain measur'd will appear
A garden to't.

SIR MAURICE. You shall be ador'd there
As goddesses.

SIR JOHN. Your litters made of gold
Supported by your vassals, proud to bear
The burden on their shoulders.

PLENTY. Pomp and ease, 120
With delicates that Europe never knew,
Like pages shall wait on you.

LUKE. If you have minds
To entertain the greatness offer'd to you,
With outstretched arms and willing hands embrace it.

---

100. *competence*] cf. IV.i.99.

But this refus'd, imagine what can make you   125
Most miserable here, and rest assur'd,
In storms it falls upon you. Take 'em in,
And use your best persuasion. If that fail,
I'll send 'em aboard in a dry fat.
    Exeunt [Sir Maurice] Lacy, Plenty, Lady [Frugal], Anne, Mary.

SIR JOHN.   Be not mov'd, sir;
We'll work 'em to your will. Yet e'er we part,   130
Your worldly cares deferr'd, a little mirth
Would not misbecome us.

LUKE.   You say well. And now
It comes into my memory, this is my birthday,
Which with solemnity I would observe,
But that it would ask cost.

SIR JOHN.   That shall not grieve you.   135
By my art I will prepare you such a feast,
As Persia in her height of pomp and riot
Die never equal; and ravishing music
As the Italian princes seldom heard
At their greatest entertainments. Name your guests.   140

LUKE.
I must have none.

SIR JOHN.   Not the city senate?

LUKE.   No;
Nor yet poor neighbors. The first would argue me
Of foolish ostentation; the latter
Of too much hospitality, and a virtue
Grown obsolete and useless. I will sit   145
Alone, and surfeit in my store, while others
With envy pine at it; my genius pamper'd
With the thought of what I am, and what they suffer
I have mark'd out to misery.

SIR JOHN.   You shall;
And something I will add, you yet conceive not,   150
Nor will I be slow-pac'd.

LUKE.   I have one business,
And that dispatch'd I am free.

_____

129. *a dry fat*] i.e., a vat.

SIR JOHN.   About it, sir,
   Leave the rest to me.
LUKE.   Till now I ne'er lov'd magic.   *Exeunt.*

[V.ii]
        Enter Lord [Lacy], Old Goldwire, *and* Old Tradewell.

LORD LACY.
        Believe me, gentlemen! I never was
        So cozen'd in a fellow. He disguis'd
        Hypocrisy in such a cunning shape
        Of real goodness, that I would have sworn
        This devil a saint. Master Goldwire, and Master Tradewell,   5
        What do you mean to do? Put on.
OLD GOLDWIRE.   With your lordship's favor.
LORD LACY.
        I'll have it so.
OLD TRADEWELL.   Your will, my lord, excuses
        The rudeness of our manners.
LORD LACY.   You have receiv'd
        Penitent letters from your sons, I doubt not?
OLD TRADEWELL.
        They are our only sons.
OLD GOLDWIRE.   And as we are fathers,   10
        Rememb'ring the errors of our youth,
        We would pardon slips in them.
OLD TRADEWELL.   And pay for 'em
        In a moderate way.
OLD GOLDWIRE.   In which we hope your lordship
        Will be our mediator.
LORD LACY.   All my power

        Enter Luke [*richly dressed*].

        You freely shall command. 'Tis he! You are well met,   15
        And to my wish—and wondrous brave! Your habit
        Speaks you a merchant royal.
LUKE.   What I wear,

---

   6. *Put on*] i.e., put your hat on.
   16. *to my wish*] as I could wish.

I take not upon trust.

LORD LACY.   Your betters may,
And blush not for't.

LUKE.   If you have nought else
With me but to argue that, I will make bold   20
To leave you.

LORD LACY.   You are very peremptory;
Pray you stay. I once held you an upright
Honest man.

LUKE.   I am honester now
By a hundred thousand pound, I thank my stars for't,
Upon the Exchange; and if your late opinion   25
Be alter'd, who can help it? Good my lord,
To the point. I have other business than to talk
Of honesty and opinions.

LORD LACY.   Yet you may
Do well, if you please, to show the one, and merit
The other from good men, in a case that now   30
Is offer'd to you.

LUKE.   What is't? I am troubl'd.

LORD LACY.
Here are two gentlemen, the fathers of
Your brother's prentices.

LUKE.   Mine, my lord, I take it.

LORD LACY.
Master Goldwire, and Master Tradewell.

LUKE.   They are welcome,
If they come prepar'd to satisfy the damage   35
I have sustain'd by their sons.

OLD GOLDWIRE.   We are, so you please
To use a conscience.

OLD TRADEWELL.   Which we hope you will do,
For your own worship's sake.

LUKE.   Conscience, my friends,
And wealth, are not always neighbors. Should I part
With what the law gives me, I should suffer mainly   40
In my reputation. For it would convince me

---

18. *trust*] credit.   41. *convince*] convict.

Of indiscretion. Nor will you, I hope, move me
To do myself such prejudice.

LORD LACY.   No moderation?

LUKE.

They cannot look for't, and preserve in me
A thriving citizen's credit. Your bonds lie   45
For your sons' truth, and they shall answer all
They have run out. The masters never prosper'd
Since gentlemen's sons grew prentices. When we look
To have our business done at home, they are
Abroad in the tennis court, or in Partridge-alley,   50
In Lambeth Marsh, or a cheating ordinary
·Where I found your sons. I have your bonds, look to't.
A thousand pounds apiece, and that will hardly
Repair my losses.

LORD LACY.   Thou dar'st not show thyself
Such a devil!

LUKE.   Good words.

LORD LACY.   Such a cutthroat! I have heard   55
Of the usage of your brother's wife and daughters.
You shall find you are not lawless, and that your moneys
Cannot justify your villanies.

LUKE.   I endure this.
And, good my lord, now you talk in time of moneys,
Pay in what you owe me. And give me leave to wonder   60
Your wisdom should have leisure to consider
The business of these gentlemen, or my carriage
To my sister, or my nieces, being yourself
So much in my danger.

LORD LACY.   In thy danger?

LUKE.   Mine.
I find in my countinghouse a manor pawn'd,   65

_____

50. *Partridge-alley*] a haunt of loose women, lying on the south side of
Holborn, near Lincoln's Inn Fields.
51. *Lambeth Marsh*] the low swampy tract on the south bank of the
Thames between Lambeth Church and Blackfriars, "notorious as the
haunts of thieves and prostitutes, sharpers and coiners" (Wheatley).

Pawn'd, my good lord, Lacy Manor, and that manor
From which you have the title of a lord,
And it please your good lordship. You are a noble man,
Pray you pay in my moneys. The interest
Will eat faster in't, than aquafortis in iron.   70
Now though you bear me hard, I love your lordship.
I grant your person to be privileg'd
From all arrests. Yet there lives a foolish creature
Call'd an under-sheriff, who being well paid, will serve
An extent on lords or lowns' land. Pay it in;   75
I would be loath your name should sink, or that
Your hopeful son, when he returns from travel,
Should find you my lord without land. You are angry
For my good counsel. Look you to your bonds; had I known
Of your coming, believe it I would have had sergeants
    ready.   80
Lord how you fret! but that a tavern's near
You should taste a cup of muscadine in my house,
To wash down sorrow, but there it will do better;
I know you'll drink a health to me.   *Exit* Luke.

LORD LACY.   To thy damnation.
Was there ever such a villain! Heaven forgive me   85
For speaking so unchristianly, though he deserves it.

OLD GOLDWIRE.
We are undone.

OLD TRADEWELL.   Our families quite ruin'd.

LORD LACY.
Take courage, gentlemen. Comfort may appear,
And punishment overtake him, when he least expects it.
                                                    Exeunt.

69–70.] *Q contains marginal S.D.*
"Plenty ready to/ speak within."

---

70. *aquafortis*] "a Liquor made of a Mixture of equal Quantities of *Salt-petre, Vitriol,* and *Potters Earth,* distilled in a close reverberating Furnace" (Bailey).
75. *An extent*] a writ whereby the body, goods, and lands of the debtor may all be taken at once to satisfy a judgment.
75. *lown*] a variant spelling of "loon," a man of lowly birth.

[V.iii]   *Enter* Sir John [Frugal], *and* Holdfast.

SIR JOHN.
    Be silent on your life.
HOLDFAST.   I am o'erjoy'd.
SIR JOHN.
    Are the pictures plac'd as I directed?
HOLDFAST.   Yes, sir.
SIR JOHN.
    And the musicians ready?
HOLDFAST.   All is done
    As you commanded.
SIR JOHN.   Make haste, and be careful;   *At the door.*
    You know your cue, and postures?
PLENTY (*within*).   We are perfect.   5
SIR JOHN.
    'Tis well. The rest are come too?
HOLDFAST.   And dispos'd of
    To your own wish.
SIR JOHN.   Set forth the table. So.

                 Enter servants with a rich banquet.

    A perfect banquet. At the upper end,
    His chair in state, he shall feast like a prince.
HOLDFAST.
    And rise like a Dutch hangman.

                      Enter Luke.

SIR JOHN.   Not a word more.—   10
    How like you the preparation? Fill your room,
    And taste the cates; then in your thought consider
    A rich man, that lives wisely to himself,
    In his full height of glory.
LUKE.   I can brook

4. *At the door.*] *after* commanded (*l.* 4)   8–10.] *Q contains marginal S.D.* "A
Q.   table, and/ rich Ban-/ quet."

10. *Dutch*] drunken (popular opinion having it that the Dutch were
excessive drinkers).
12. *cates*] delicacies.

No rival in this happiness. How sweetly   15
These dainties, when unpaid for, please my palate!
Some wine. Jove's nectar! Brightness to the star
That govern'd at my birth. Shoot down thy influence,
And with a perpetuity of being
Continue this felicity, not gain'd   20
By vows to saints above, and much less purchas'd
By thriving industry; nor fall'n upon me
As a reward to piety and religion,
Or service for my country. I owe all this
To dissimulation, and the shape   25
I wore of goodness. Let my brother number
His beads devoutly, and believe his alms
To beggars, his compassion to his debtors,
Will wing his better part, disrob'd of flesh,
To soar above the firmament. I am well,   30
And so I surfeit here in all abundance,
Though styl'd a cormorant, a cutthroat, Jew,
And prosecuted with the fatal curses
Of widows, undone orphans, and what else
Such as malign my state can load me with,   35
I will not envy it. You promis'd music?

SIR JOHN.

And you shall hear the strength and power
Of it, the spirit of Orpheus rais'd to make it good,
And in those ravishing strains with which he mov'd
Charon and Cerberus to give him way   40
To fetch from hell his lost Eurydice.
—Appear swifter than thought.

Music. [*Enter*] *at one door* Cerberus, *at the other* Charon, Orpheus,
Chorus.

LUKE.   'Tis wondrous strange.
                          [*They mime the story of Orpheus.*]

SIR JOHN.

Does not the object and the accent take you?

22. By thriving] *Dodsley;* By the
thriving *Q.*

LUKE.

    A pretty fable.

                              [Exeunt Orpheus *and the rest.]*
                But that music should
Alter in fiends their nature, is to me   45
Impossible; since in myself I find
What I have once decreed shall know no change.

SIR JOHN.

    You are constant to your purposes, yet I think
That I could stagger you.

LUKE.   How?

SIR JOHN.   Should I present
Your servants, debtors, and the rest that suffer   50
By your fit severity, I presume the sight
Would move you to compassion.

LUKE.   Not a mote.
The music that your Orpheus made was harsh,
To the delight I should receive in hearing
Their cries and groans. If it be in your power,   55
I would now see 'em.

SIR JOHN.   Spirits in their shapes
Shall show them as they are. But if it should move you?

LUKE.

    If it do, may I ne'er find pity.

SIR JOHN.

    Be your own judge. —Appear as I commanded.

Sad music. Enter [Young] Goldwire *and* [Young] Tradewell, *as from prison;* Fortune, Hoyst, Penury *following after them;* Shave'em *in a blue gown;* Secret, Ding'em, Old Tradewell, *and* Old Goldwire *with* Sergeants. *As directed they all kneel to* Luke, *heaving up their hands for mercy;* Stargaze *with a pack of almanacs,* Milliscent.

LUKE.

    Ha, ha, ha!   60
This move me to compassion, or raise
One sign of seeming pity in my face?

44. S.D.] *Gifford; not in* Q.   45. fiends] *Dodsley;* friends Q.
44–45.] *Q contains marginal S.D.* 59.4. directed] *Dodsley; erected* Q.
"*Plenty and| Lacie ready behind.*"

You are deceiv'd. It rather renders me
More flinty, and obdurate. A south wind
Shall sooner soften marble, and the rain   65
That slides down gently from his flaggy wings
O'erflow the Alps, than knees or tears or groans
Shall wrest compunction from me. 'Tis my glory
That they are wretched, and by me made so;
It sets my happiness off. I could not triumph   70
If these were not my captives. Ha! my terriers
As it appears have seiz'd on these old foxes,
As I gave order. New addition to
My scene of mirth. Ha! ha! They now grow tedious.
Let 'em be remov'd. Some other object, if   75
Your art can show it.   [*Exeunt* Young Goldwire *and the rest.*]
SIR JOHN.   You shall perceive 'tis boundless.
Yet one thing real, if you please?
LUKE.   What is it?
SIR JOHN.
Your nieces, e'er they put to sea, crave humbly,
Though absent in their bodies, they may take leave
Of their late suitors' statues.

          Enter Lady [Frugal], Anne, *and* Mary.

LUKE.   There they hang;   80
In things indifferent, I am tractable.
SIR JOHN.
There pay your vows; you have liberty.
ANNE.   O sweet figure
Of my abused Lacy! when remov'd
Into another world, I'll daily pay
A sacrifice of sighs to thy remembrance;   85
And with a shower of tears strive to wash off
The stain of that contempt my foolish pride
And insolence threw upon thee.
MARY.   I had been
Too happy if I had enjoy'd the substance,

81. indifferent] *Dodsley;* different *Q*   86. off] *Dodsley;* of *Q.*

---

80. *statues*] "loosely used for: Image, effigy" (*OED*).

But far unworthy of it, now I fall   90
Thus prostrate to thy statue.

LADY FRUGAL.   My kind husband,
Blessed in my misery, from the monastery
To which my disobedience confin'd thee,
With thy soul's eye, which distance cannot hinder,
Look on my penitence. O, that I could   95
Call back time past! thy holy vow dispens'd,
With what humility would I observe
My long-neglected duty.

SIR JOHN.   Does not this move you?

LUKE.
Yes, as they do the statues, and her sorrow
My absent brother. If by your magic art   100
You can give life to these, or bring him hither
To witness her repentance, I may have
Perchance some feeling of it.

SIR JOHN.   For your sport
You shall see a masterpiece. Here's nothing but
A superficies—colors, and no substance.   105
Sit still, and to your wonder and amazement
I'll give these organs. This the sacrifice
To make the great work perfect.

[*Burns incense, and makes mystical gesticulations.* Sir Maurice Lacy *and*
Plenty *give signs of animation.*]

LUKE.   Prodigious!

SIR JOHN.
Nay, they have life and motion. Descend.
            [Sir Maurice Lacy *and* Plenty *descend and come forward.*]
And for your absent brother— This wash'd off,   110
Against your will you shall know him.   [*Discovers himself.*]

                    Enter Lord [Lacy] *and the rest.*

LUKE.   I am lost.

90. fall] *Mason;* shall *Q*.   109.1. *Gifford; not in Q*.
108. S.D.] *Gifford; Enter Lacie and*   111. S.D. *Discovers himself.*] *Gifford;*
Plenty. Q.   *not in Q*.

_____

    105. *superficies*] outward form.

Guilt strikes me dumb.
SIR JOHN.   You have seen, my lord, the pageant?
LORD LACY.
 I have, and am ravish'd with it.
SIR JOHN.   What think you now
 Of this clear soul? this honest, pious man?
 Have I stripp'd him bare? Or will your lordship have 115
 A farther trial of him? 'Tis not in
 A wolf to change his nature.
LORD LACY.   I long since
 Confess'd my error.
SIR JOHN.   Look up, I forgive you,
 And seal your pardons thus.
    [*Raises and embraces* Lady Frugal, Anne, *and* Mary.]
LADY FRUGAL.   I am too full
 Of joy to speak it.
ANNE.   I am another creature, 120
 Not what I was.
MARY.   I vow to show myself,
 When I am married, an humble wife,
 Not a commanding mistress.
PLENTY.   On those terms,
 I gladly thus embrace you.
SIR MAURICE [*to* Anne].   Welcome to
 My bosom. As the one half of myself, 125
 I'll love you, and cherish you.
YOUNG GOLDWIRE.   Mercy!
YOUNG TRADEWELL *and the rest*.   Good sir, mercy!
SIR JOHN.
 This day is sacred to it. All shall find me,
 As far as lawful pity can give way to 't,
 Indulgent to your wishes, though with loss
 Unto myself. My kind and honest brother, 130
 Looking into yourself, have you seen the Gorgon?
 What a golden dream you have had in the possession
 Of my estate!—but here's a revocation
 That wakes you out of it. Monster in nature!

119. S.D.] *Gifford; not in Q.*

Revengeful, avaricious atheist,   135
Transcending all example! But I shall be
A sharer in thy crimes, should I repeat 'em.
What wilt thou do? Turn hypocrite again,
With hope dissimulation can aid thee?
Or that one eye will shed a tear in sign   140
Of sorrow for thee? I have warrant to
Make bold with mine own, pray you uncase. This key, too,
I must make bold with. Hide thyself in some desert,
Where good men ne'er may find thee: or in justice
Pack to Virginia, and repent; not for   145
Those horrid ends to which thou did'st design these.

LUKE.
I care not where I go; what's done with words
Cannot be undone.   *Exit* Luke.

LADY FRUGAL.   Yet, sir, show some mercy;
Because his cruelty to me, and mine,
Did good upon us.

SIR JOHN.   Of that at better leisure,   150
As his penitency shall work me. Make you good
Your promis'd reformation, and instruct
Our city dames, whom wealth makes proud, to move
In their spheres, and willingly to confess
In their habits, manners, and their highest port,   155
A distance 'twixt the city and the court.   *Exeunt omnes.*

FINIS

152. instruct] *Dodsley;* mistrust *Q*.

Appendix

Chronology

Approximate years are indicated by *, occurrences in doubt by (?).

Political and Literary Events	Life and Major Works of Massinger

1558
Accession of Queen Elizabeth.
Robert Greene born.
Thomas Kyd born.

1560
George Chapman born.

1561
Francis Bacon born.

1564
Shakespeare born.
Christopher Marlowe born.

1570
Thomas Heywood born.*

1572
Thomas Dekker born.*
John Donne born.
Massacre of St. Bartholomew's Day.

1573
Ben Jonson born.*

1576
The Theatre, the first permanent public theater in London, established by James Burbage.
John Marston born.

1577
The Curtain theater opened.
Holinshed's *Chronicles of England, Scotland and Ireland.*
Drake begins circumnavigation of the earth; completed 1580.

1579
John Fletcher born.
John Lyly's *Euphues: The Anatomy of Wit* published.
Sir Thomas North's translation of Plutarch's *Lives*.

1580
Thomas Middleton born.

1583

Philip Massinger baptized at St. Thomas's, Salisbury, November 24.

1584
Francis Beaumont born.*

1586
Death of Sir Philip Sidney.
John Ford born.

1587
The Rose theater opened by Henslowe.
Marlowe's *TAMBURLAINE*, Part I.*
Execution of Mary, Queen of Scots.
Drake raids Cadiz.

1588
Defeat of the Spanish Armada.
Marlowe's *TAMBURLAINE*, Part II.*

1589
Greene's *FRIAR BACON AND FRIAR BUNGAY*.*
Marlowe's *THE JEW OF MALTA*.*
Kyd's *THE SPANISH TRAGEDY*.*

1590
Spenser's *Faerie Queene* (Books I–III) published.
Sidney's *Arcadia* published.
Shakespeare's *HENRY VI*, Parts I–III,* *TITUS ANDRONICUS*.*

1591
Shakespeare's *RICHARD III*.*

1592

Marlowe's *DOCTOR FAUSTUS**
and *EDWARD II.**

Shakespeare's *TAMING OF THE
SHREW** and *THE COMEDY OF
ERRORS.**

Death of Greene.

1593

Shakespeare's *LOVE'S LABOUR'S
LOST;* Venus and Adonis* published.

Death of Marlowe.

Theaters closed on account of
plague.

1594

Shakespeare's *TWO GENTLEMEN
OF VERONA;* The Rape of Lucrece*
published.

Shakespeare's company becomes
Lord Chamberlain's Men.

James Shirley born.*

Death of Kyd.

1595

The Swan theater built.

Sidney's *Defense of Poesy* published.

Shakespeare's *ROMEO AND
JULIET,* A MIDSUMMER
NIGHT'S DREAM,* RICHARD
II.**

Raleigh's first expedition to Guiana.

1596

Spenser's *Faerie Queene* (Books IV–
VI) published.

Shakespeare's *MERCHANT OF
VENICE,* KING JOHN.**

1597

Bacon's *Essays* (first edition).

Shakespeare's *HENRY IV*, Part I.*

1598

Demolition of the Theatre.

Shakespeare's *MUCH ADO
ABOUT NOTHING,* HENRY IV,*
Part II.*

Jonson's *EVERY MAN IN HIS HUMOR* (first version).

Seven books of Chapman's translation of Homer's *Iliad* published.

1599

The Globe theater opened.

Shakespeare's *AS YOU LIKE IT,** *HENRY V,** *JULIUS CAESAR,** Dekker's *THE SHOEMAKERS' HOLIDAY.**

Death of Spenser.

1600

Shakespeare's *TWELFTH NIGHT,** *HAMLET.**

Marston's *ANTONIO AND MELLIDA,** *ANTONIO'S REVENGE.**

The Fortune theater built by Alleyn.

1601

Shakespeare's *MERRY WIVES OF WINDSOR.**

Insurrection and execution of the Earl of Essex.

1602

Shakespeare's *TROILUS AND CRESSIDA,** *ALL'S WELL THAT ENDS WELL.**

Matriculates at St. Alban Hall, Oxford, May 14.

1603

Death of Queen Elizabeth; accession of James VI of Scotland as James I.

Florio's translation of Montaigne's *Essays* published.

Heywood's *A WOMAN KILLED WITH KINDNESS.*

Marston's *THE MALCONTENT.**

Shakespeare's company becomes the King's Men.

1604

Shakespeare's *MEASURE FOR MEASURE,** *OTHELLO.**

Marston's *THE FAWN.**

Chapman's *BUSSY D'AMBOIS.**

1605
Shakespeare's *KING LEAR.**
Marston's *THE DUTCH COUR-
TEZAN.**
Bacon's *Advancement of Learning*
published.
The Gunpowder Plot.

1606
Shakespeare's *MACBETH.**
Jonson's *VOLPONE.**
Tourneur's *REVENGER'S TRAG-
EDY.**
The Red Bull theater built.
Death of John Lyly.

1607
Shakespeare's *ANTONY AND
CLEOPATRA.**
Beaumont's *KNIGHT OF THE
BURNING PESTLE.**
Settlement of Jamestown, Virginia.

1608
Shakespeare's *CORIOLANUS,**
*TIMON OF ATHENS,** *PERI-
CLES.**
Chapman's *CONSPIRACY AND
TRAGEDY OF CHARLES, DUKE
OF BYRON.**
Dekker's *Gull's Hornbook* pub-
lished.
Richard Burbage leases Blackfriars
Theatre for King's Company.
John Milton born.

1609
Shakespeare's *CYMBELINE;** *Son-
nets* published.
Jonson's *EPICOENE.*

1610
Jonson's *ALCHEMIST.*
Chapman's *REVENGE OF BUSSY
D'AMBOIS.**
Richard Crashaw born.

1611

Authorized (King James) Version
of the Bible published.
Shakespeare's *THE WINTER'S
TALE,* * THE TEMPEST.* *
Beaumont and Fletcher's *A KING
AND NO KING.*
Tourneur's *ATHEIST'S TRAG-
EDY.* *
Chapman's translation of *Iliad*
completed.

1612

Webster's *THE WHITE DEVIL.* *

1613

The Globe theater burned.
Shakespeare's *HENRY VIII* (with
Fletcher).
Webster's *THE DUCHESS OF
MALFI.* *
Middleton's *A CHASTE MAID IN
CHEAPSIDE.*
Sir Thomas Overbury murdered.

Collaborates with Field and Daborne in an unspecified play for
Henslowe.*

1614

The Globe theater rebuilt.
The Hope Theatre built.
Jonson's *BARTHOLOMEW FAIR.*

1615

With Daborne, signs a bond on
July 4 for the payment of three
pounds to Henslowe on the first of
August following.

1616

Publication of Folio edition of
Jonson's *Works.*
Death of Shakespeare.
Death of Beaumont.

Begins writing regularly (though
not exclusively) for the King's
Company.*
Collaborates with Fletcher and
Field in *THE JEWELLER OF
AMSTERDAM* (now lost).*

1617

THE KNIGHT OF MALTA, *
THE QUEEN OF CORINTH *
(both with Fletcher and Field).

1618
Outbreak of Thirty Years War.
Execution of Raleigh.

THE OLD LAW (with Middleton and Rowley).*

1619

THE FATAL DOWRY (with Field).*
SIR JOHN VAN OLDEN BARNA-VELT (with Fletcher).

1620
Pilgrim Fathers land at Plymouth.

THE VIRGIN MARTYR (with Dekker).*
THE CUSTOM OF THE COUNTRY, *THE FALSE ONE* (both with Fletcher).

1621
Middleton's *WOMEN BEWARE WOMEN.**
Robert Burton's *Anatomy of Melancholy* published.
Andrew Marvell born.

*THE MAID OF HONOR,** *A NEW WAY TO PAY OLD DEBTS.**
THE DOUBLE MARRIAGE (with Fletcher).*

1622
Middleton and Rowley's *THE CHANGELING.**
Henry Vaughan born.

*THE DUKE OF MILAN.**
With Fletcher: *THE PROPHET-ESS, THE SEA VOYAGE,** *THE SPANISH CURATE.**

1623
Publication of Folio edition of Shakespeare's *COMEDIES, HIS-TORIES, AND TRAGEDIES.*

THE BONDMAN.
THE LITTLE FRENCH LAWYER (with Fletcher).*

1624

THE PARLIAMENT OF LOVE, THE RENEGADO.

1625
Death of King James I; accession of Charles I.
Death of Fletcher.

*THE UNNATURAL COMBAT.**
THE FAIR MAID OF THE INN (with Fletcher, Webster, and Ford).

1626
Death of Tourneur.
Death of Bacon.

THE ROMAN ACTOR.

1627
Death of Middleton.

*THE GREAT DUKE OF FLORENCE.** *THE JUDGE* (lost).

1628
Ford's *THE LOVER'S MELAN-CHOLY*.
Petition of Right.
Buckingham assassinated.
1629

THE PICTURE. MINERVA'S SACRIFICE (lost).

1631
Shirley's *THE TRAITOR*.
Death of Donne.

BELIEVE AS YOU LIST, THE EMPEROR OF THE EAST. THE UNFORTUNATE PIETY (lost).

1632
Death of Dekker.*

*THE CITY MADAM.**

1633
Donne's *Poems* published.
Death of George Herbert.

THE GUARDIAN.

1634
Death of Chapman, Marston, Webster.*
THE TWO NOBLE KINSMEN published.

Revision of Fletcher's *THE LOVERS' PROGRESS* as *CLEANDER.**
Revision of Fletcher's *A VERY WOMAN*.

1635
Sir Thomas Brown's *Religio Medici*.

Revision of Fletcher's *THE ELDER BROTHER.**
THE ORATOR (lost).

1636

THE BASHFUL LOVER.

1637
Death of Jonson
1638

THE KING AND THE SUBJECT (lost).

1639
First Bishops' War.
Death of Carew.*

ALEXIUS, OR THE CHASTE LOVER (lost).

1640
Short Parliament.
Long Parliament impeaches Laud.
Death of Burton.

THE FAIR ANCHORESS OF PAUSILIPPO (lost).
Massinger dies in London, and is buried on March 18.